Collins

pony
handbook

DAVID TAYLOR
BVMS, FRCVS, FZS

David Taylor is a well-known veterinary surgeon and broadcaster and the author of over thirty books, including six volumes of autobiography, some of which formed the basis for three series of the BBC television drama *One by One*.

He has also written *Collins Small Pet Handbook* and *Collins Family Pet Guides*: *Rabbit*. The founder of the International Zoo Veterinary Group, he has exotic patients across the world, ranging from crocodiles to killer whales and giant pandas. He lives in Richmond, Surrey, with his wife and five cats.

pony
handbook

David Taylor
BVMS, FRCVS, FZS

First published in 2002 by
HarperCollins*Publishers*
77–85 Fulham Palace Road
Hammersmith
London W6 8JB

The HarperCollins website address is
www.**fire**and**water**.com

Collins is a registered trademark of
HarperCollins Publishers Limited.

07 06 05 04 03 02
9 8 7 6 5 4 3 2 1

Text, design and illustrations
© HarperCollinsPublishers Ltd, 2002
Photographs © HarperCollinsPublishers,
Houghtons Horses, 2002

A catalogue record of this book is available from
the British Library.

ISBN 0 00 712092 3

This book was created by
SP Creative Design
Sarah's Folly, Grange Road, Wickham Skeith,
Suffolk IP23 8NF
EDITOR: **HEATHER THOMAS**
ART DIRECTOR AND PRODUCTION: **ROLANDO UGOLINI**
PHOTOGRAPHY: **ROLANDO UGOLINI**
ADDITIONAL PHOTOGRAPHY:
Kit Houghton: pages 14 and 18–29

Colour reproduction by Colourscan, Singapore
Printed and bound by Printing Express Ltd, Hong Kong

CONTENTS

INTRODUCTION

Almost every one of the multitude of folk across the world who takes to the saddle every year began his or her peculiar relationship with *Equus* by way of one of the smallest representations of the horse family, the pony. The jockeys in the Belmont Stakes or the Grand National, the outback farmer doing the rounds of his stock, the mounted policeman; all these, and millions more, in most cases started riding on a little, often impish, sometimes downright wilful horselet.

In Britain and elsewhere in the Western world, ponies and pony riding are increasing steadily in popularity. Pony clubs thrive in town suburbs, city centres and the countryside; pony trekking holidays across the uplands attract ever more enthusiasts; and each day as I drive around (in a car, not a pony trap, I sadly confess), the number of cheerful youngsters mounted on rascally Thelwell look-alikes seems to increase. Methods of transport for pulling and carrying they may be, but ponies are far more complex and wonderful than that. They are more than pets, more than a hobby or a pastime, more than mere beasts of burden. Ponies are philosophers and companions, confidants and friends. Ponies are magic.

This book is for the amateur, the dabbler, the beginner and all those lucky individuals who are falling firmly under the spell of the most superior of domesticated animals.

CHAPTER ONE

EVOLUTION AND BREEDS

Ponies developed over the aeons in ways that were quite different from those of other groups of herbivores. Their bodies adapted to digest the cellulose-containing plant material that was now abundant on the dry land of the earth. And to protect themselves from dangerous, non-herbivorous predators, the biological process of natural selection produced their characteristic speed and nimbleness, their sharp reactions and highly tuned senses. Only much later, when man arrived upon the scene and recognized their potential for domestication, did artificial selection, the breeding of equines to create types for specialized forms of work, begin.

EVOLUTION OF THE PONY

About 55 million years ago, in what are now called Europe and North America but which were then joined together in one land-mass, a little dog-like animal moved through the forests, browsing on low shrubs. This was *Hyracotherium*, ancestor of the horse and also of the rhinoceros and tapirs. Descended itself from forebears possessing the basic five toes per foot, it had already lost two outer toes on its hind feet and one inner toe on its fore feet, the remaining toes looking dog-like, with pads; there was no sign of hooves as yet. It had a short muzzle and a long tail curved like a cat's.

As the aeons passed, the descendants of *Hyracotherium* split off into numerous branches of the family tree. The rhinos and tapirs went their way; the equine branch went theirs, discarding more toes so that they might concentrate on the perfection of a single, highly modified toe on each foot, growing larger, developing teeth which were ideal for cropping and grinding grass, and acquiring large, efficient eyes.

By about one million years ago, all the surviving equine descendants of the original *Hyracotherium* had settled into four main groups: the horses, the asses, the half-asses and the zebras. They were distributed (as shown in the diagram) in fairly specific parts of Africa, Europe and the Middle East, with almost no overlapping of the various groups. The zebras were purely southern African and the half-asses (ancestors of the onager, kulan, kiang and djiggetai, and of the hemione which became extinct about a hundred years ago) were all Asiatic. The asses, from which donkeys were developed, were purely northern African, and the horses (including ponies, which are simply horses under 14.2 hands high) were inhabitants of Europe and of western Asia.

By the Ice Age, scientists could identify four major types of horse or pony existing in the world and, with the disappearance of all horses in the Americas by about 6000 BC (being reintroduced much later by the Spanish conquistadors), this means solely in Europe and western Asia. The cause of the horse's demise in the Americas is the subject of much speculation. Changes in climate or food availability were probably not involved for other large herbivores, such as the bison, survived and prospered. Some scientists believe that a virulent viral or protozoal disease, probably carried by insects, may have swept across the continent killing the equines, but the reason remains one of the great unsolved mysteries.

EQUINE DISTRIBUTION OVER THE LAST ONE MILLION YEARS

Continents originally joined here

Horses

Horses

Half-asses

Asses

Zebras

THE FOUR TYPES OF PONY

From the four types, our modern horse and pony breeds are descended.

🔺 **Type 1** was a pony of north-western Europe, standing about 12.2 hands and in many respects very similar to the Exmoor ponies of today.

🔺 **Type 2** was also a pony but heavier than type 1. Its height was up to 14.2 hands and its coat was lighter-coloured. Most of the European horses of the early Stone Age seem to have been of this type. It most closely resembled the Przewalski horse of today.

🔺 **Type 3** was a central Asian horse of around 15 hands. This long-headed equine did not apparently play a significant part in later horse and pony evolution.

🔺 **Type 4** was strictly a pony, although it is often referred to as a fine-boned small horse. It grew up to 12 hands and lived in western Asia. The modern pony that most closely resembles it is the Caspian pony from Iran.

Modern ponies are generally thought to be made up from crossings between some or all of the four types. Crosses between types 1 and 4 probably led to the tarpan, a wild horse that survived in Russia, eastern Europe and Germany until the nineteenth century. (By selecting breeds that possibly most closely resemble the tarpan, such as Icelandic ponies and Gotland horses, crossing them through several generations, it has been possible to 're-create' the extinct animal in recent years.) The tarpan is an ancestor of many pony breeds that we know today, including the Konik of Poland, the Bosnian pony of Yugoslavia, the Hucul of the Carpathian mountains and the Scweike of Poland.

BELOW: *Our modern pony breeds have all evolved from the earliest types of pony. They come in a variety of different sizes, coat types and colours.*

DOMESTICATION

This began around 3000 BC, almost certainly in eastern Europe (the Ukrainian and Russian steppes), Kazakhstan and in the steppes of western Asia, mainly around Lake Aral. From these areas, the domestic equine spread outwards after 2000 BC, although the Sumerians had also been domesticating onagers as early as 3000 BC in what is now Iraq. Type 2 was the first to be domesticated for riding and pack work, probably by reindeer herdsmen. Following that, types 4 and then 3 were broken for harnessing to chariots. Finally type 1 was tamed, originally to be used as a pack animal since asses and mules were unknown to Europeans north of the Alps before about AD 100. Before 600 BC, all the 'horses' ridden or driven by ancient civilizations were in fact ponies!

All 'wild' ponies (excluding the Przewalski horse) which exist today and including the nine British breeds (see pages 18–23), should really be called 'feral': descendants of the domesticated stock that went back to the wild. The brumbies of Australia, many of which are annually trapped, slaughtered and processed for pet food, are descended from domestic ponies imported by the settlers and have been breeding in the wild for over 130 years. Some experts consider that certain breeds of British pony might have some truly wild blood in them. The Exmoor just might be a true-blooded wild pony inhabiting a part of Britain that escaped the glaciation of the Ice Age, and there is speculation, too, about the Connemaras. Although the latter certainly has much Arab blood in it, horse skulls have been found in Irish peat bogs dating from a time just after the Ice Age and before domesticated horses are thought to have been used in Ireland.

LEFT: *The fortunes of the pony have greatly changed in Western countries. Once a beast of burden, now it is valued for its companionship and its important role in recreational riding.*

INTERBREEDING

Under natural conditions, wild equine species do not seem to interbreed. Even mountain zebras never cross with Butchell's zebras living in the same area. Grevy's zebras don't cross with wild asses in Somalia, nor onagers with Przewalski horses in Mongolia. Among domesticated animals, however, crosses do occur:

🔺 Male donkey x horse mare = mule
🔺 Female donkey x horse stallion = hinny
🔺 Zebra x horse = zebroid.

All these hybrids, except for the occasional mule and zebra cross, are generally sterile although they are strong, amenable creatures. On the very rare occasions when they do breed successfully, a female mule crossed with a horse stallion produces either a mule or a horse; and the offspring of a female mule/male donkey cross will be either a proper mule or a proper ass. They never produce anything in between, because some of the eggs formed by the mule ovary are pure horse ones and others are pure donkey eggs. The eggs themselves are never hybrids.

ABOVE: *Many young enthusiasts get their first taste of equine pleasures from the humble, delightful donkey.*

THE QUAGGA

Within living memory, one of the pony's wild relatives, a lovely, mysterious creature that looked half-zebra, half-pony, was made extinct by guess who? Man. This was the quagga of the South African plains. It had dark brown stripes on its head and neck, a brown body and white legs and belly. Although claims to have seen specimens continued until as late as 1920, it is fairly certain that the last wild quagga was shot in 1861. They were said to emit a shrill bark.

Quaggas in captivity had thrived well – one was kept at Windsor Castle in the 1820s, and in 1860 a team of quaggas pulled a feed cart round London Zoo. The last quagga at Regent's Park died in 1872, and the last quagga in the world died in Amsterdam in 1883. Incredibly, but not uniquely (as witness the passing of the American passenger pigeon), no-one attempted to breed quaggas in captivity; I suppose they assumed there would always be an abundance of wild quaggas in Africa. There are photographs of quaggas in existence, and also the famous Stubbs painting of a quagga in the Royal College of Surgeons. About 20 quagga skins collect dust in the museums of the world. Let's hope that the wild horses and asses still clinging on to a precarious existence don't end up like that.

PIT PONIES

Up until recent years coal mines, especially those in South Wales, used ponies underground to pull loads of coal from the pit face to the shaft. These animals lived in perpetual gloom, covered in grime and dust, but generally well treated by the miners who shared their subterranean labours with all the attendant dangers and deprivation.

Happily, there are now no more ponies living down the mines; the last ones were brought to the surface to spend the rest of their lives in fresh air and sunlight. A number of rehabilitation centres for pit ponies, such as the one at Fforest Uchai Farm, near Pontypridd in Wales, look after these doughty little animals so deserving a peaceful retirement.

ABOVE: *A most happy sight; a retired pit pony grazing in the sunlight, never to go underground ever again.*

HOW THE PONY EVOLVED

Ponies are built as we find them today, essentially because of a fundamental change in the Earth's climate which began about 24 million years ago. The weather became more distinctly and regularly seasonal, it was drier and the tropical zone contracted towards the Equator. The forests began to retreat, and everywhere the plants that we call grasses became abundant. Open savannahs of grassland were established, and to take advantage of them, the horsey descendants of *Hyracotherium* moved out of the bush. And, so that these creatures could cope with the benefits and dangers of the new wide-open spaces, evolution changed the structure of the equine body in various very sensible ways.

The three key requirements for life on the plains were as follows:

▲ Efficient implements for cropping and grinding grass which, unlike the leaves on which the forest-living ancestors had lived, contains much harsh silica as well as more tough fibre – teeth.

▲ Mechanisms for detecting trouble at a safe distance – senses.

▲ Ways of avoiding trouble, now that the protective cover of the trees was forsaken – physique.

Horses, including modern ponies and donkeys, have got all the right gear for doing these three things.

Teeth

The animals have two excellent types of teeth for dealing with grass: sharp incisors for cropping it, and special, high-crowned cheek teeth (molars and so on) for grinding it. Other grass-eaters, such as cattle, sheep and deer, digest fibrous food in their multi-chambered stomachs where they maintain colonies of useful digestive bacteria as slaves. Horses, ponies and donkeys have relatively simple stomachs much more like man's, and possess very spacious large intestines in which bacteria also aid the digestive process.

Eyes and ears

Open spaces led to the evolution of large eyes that were set on the sides of the head, perfectly positioned to watch the horizon for any hint of danger while grazing. (Excellent hearing, with mobile, 'direction-finding' ears, helps in the same way.) The pony and donkey have excellent sight and can see a man at a distance of almost one mile. As the eyes are set at the sides, the fields of vision of the two organs do not overlap and so they are unable to see stereoscopically, in 3-D, as we do. On the other hand, the horizontal, oblong pupil is the eye, which resembles a letter-box, and gives a far wider visual sweep of the distance than a round pupil would.

Although it cannot see as much of the spectrum as man and other primates, the pony does have quite a wide range of colour vision – in this respect, it is on a par with giraffes, sheep and squirrels! Ponies can see much fine detail; their zebra cousins can recognise one another by the particular pattern of their stripes. Luckily, no two zebras have identical striping.

The mobile ears are used not just to catch sounds but also, particularly in wild horses, as a means of communication. They wag them to one another in a kind of simple semaphore.

The sense of smell is first class. The nostrils are large and supple and can be closed tightly against dust or sand-storms. In a good wind, a wild ass can scent a man at 457 m/500 yd.

Physique

Ponies have a larger body size than their ancient forest-dwelling ancestors; bulkier bodies both use food and conserve heat more efficiently. This increase in size was fine for animals that no longer had to slip under low-hanging branches.

To out-distance any attackers, the equines concentrated the immense power of their body muscles onto just four toes – one on each leg. The other toes were largely discarded so that the one that was left could be specially modified for superb running by elaborating the primitive 'nail' into a hoof and devising a complex system of ligaments in the fetlock which increased flexibility on a fore-and-aft direction, decreased it from side to side and so gave the leg much extra spring.

Domesticated ponies can be fairly nippy movers but cannot rival their wild cousins. Wild asses can be remarkably swift and untiring, some experts reckoning them to be superior in some respects to riding-horses. Onagers, for example, have been timed running at an average of 45 kph/28 mph for nearly half an hour with short bursts of over 48 kph/30 mph. Compare this with the record for a thoroughbred race-horse under ideal conditions over 5 km/3 miles of 55.18 kph/34.29 mph. Even over a short distance, the racehorse is unlikely to surpass 64 kph/40 mph. The wild asses are no mean jumpers, either: onagers have cleared walls 3 m/7½ ft high!

Finally, biologists put ponies fairly high on the animal scale of intelligence, and they are also believed to possess good memories. And one thing is certain: the humblest pony is as thoroughly equipped as a Derby winner with all the refinements that enabled horses to come galloping out of the jungle so many aeons ago.

Croup

Loins

Dock

Point of hip

Point of buttock

Thigh

Gaskin

Point of hock

Flank

Sheath

Stifle

Hock

Cannon

Tendons

Pastern

Ergot

Coronet

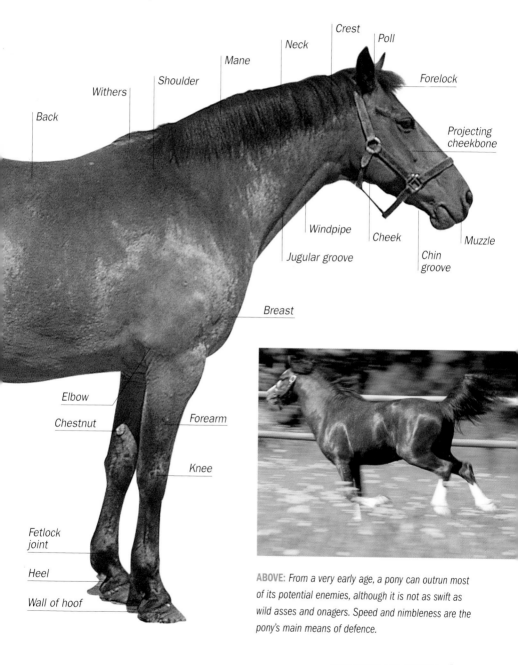

BELOW: *The points of a horse or pony; a vocabulary that every pony owner needs to possess.*

Crest

Poll

Neck

Mane

Shoulder

Forelock

Withers

Back

Projecting cheekbone

Windpipe

Cheek

Muzzle

Jugular groove

Chin groove

Breast

Elbow

Chestnut

Forearm

Knee

Fetlock joint

Heel

Wall of hoof

ABOVE: *From a very early age, a pony can outrun most of its potential enemies, although it is not as swift as wild asses and onagers. Speed and nimbleness are the pony's main means of defence.*

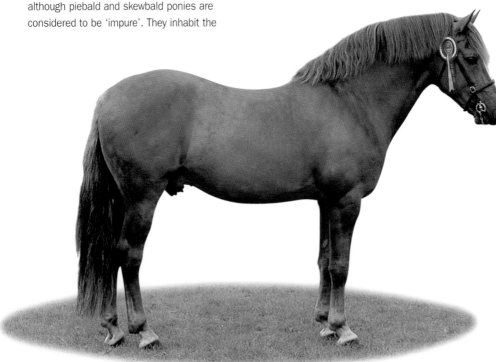

COMMON BRITISH BREEDS

At the beginning of the last century, Britain boasted fifteen or more distinct pony breeds. Some of them, such as the Galloway, disappeared within living memory although their blood lives on in many Highland and Fell ponies. Today the native pony breeds of Great Britain, usually called mountain and moorland ponies although they are by no means located solely in or adapted to the uplands, are nine in number. Stud books and regulation of standards are maintained for each breed. The nine breeds are as follows:

NEW FOREST PONIES

This breed comes in all sorts of colours, although piebald and skewbald ponies are considered to be 'impure'. They inhabit the Crown forest that gives them their name and which lies in Hampshire between the River Avon and Southampton Water. Their breeding is controlled by the selection of stallions which are caught and shown every April, inferior specimens being weeded out. The mares run free all year round, tending to stay in particular parts of the forest which can be regarded as their home, in groups of between one and six with their offspring. The ponies are good for the Forest itself; their movements and grazing stop the woodland becoming choked with undergrowth.

BELOW: *This chestnut New Forest pony stallion is a superb specimen.*

DARTMOOR PONIES

These resemble New Forest ponies but, because the stallions are not selected systematically as they are for the New Forest breed, they come in an even greater range of varieties. They have small heads with very small ears and stand between 11 and 12.2 hands. The colours are normally bay, black, brown or grey; again, piebalds and skewbalds are taboo. Dartmoor ponies are kindly folk and easily tamed.

EXMOOR PONIES

True Exmoors, unlike other British ponies, are uniform in appearance: they are dark brown in colour with little or no white. They have a light-coloured muzzle; a broad forehead; short, thick ears; nice big eyes;

ABOVE: A *Dartmoor pony stallion. Its head is somewhat smaller than those of most other pony breeds.*

BELOW: *This Exmoor pony is showing its overall uniform dark brown coat.*

a deep barrel-like chest; fine legs; and a rather harsh, springy coat. They stand about 12.2 hands high (a hand is 10 cm/ 4 in, so 12.2 hands is 125 cm/50 in). They are very rugged and have been known to survive unusually severe winters that killed off sheep and even deer. It is possible that the Exmoor is Britain's only truly pure wild horse. Some experts even consider it to be the only pure-blooded wild horse still existing in the world – this school of thought believes the Przewalski horse to be a cross-bred. Certainly the Exmoor area escaped glaciation during the Ice Age, and in the Mendip Caves have been discovered fossilized remains, dated as being around 100,000 years old and identical to modern Exmoor ponies.

CONNEMARA PONIES

This docile breed comes from the hills of Galway in Ireland. It also occurs in many colours, has a deep, 'chunky' body and short legs and stands 13–14.2 hands. Lots of Arab blood flows through its veins and it makes a doughty little jumper.

BELOW: *This Connemara pony is plainly carrying some Arab characteristics.*

WELSH PONIES

These ponies come in all colours and have a heavy head with a short mane and tail. There may be true British wild pony blood in them, but in the main they are descended from Oriental breeds which were imported by the Romans.

SHETLAND PONIES

They may be small (around 10.2 hands) but Shetlands are tough and strong. They have broad chests and hindquarters, lovely flowing manes and tails, small ears and large, well-spaced eyes. Colours are variable, but black is particularly popular. Shetlands still live out all the year round. Selective breeding and control of the type did not begin until the late nineteenth century under the auspices of Lord Londonderry in Great Britain.

ABOVE: *The doughty and reliable Shetland pony.*
BELOW: *A Welsh pony of the Welsh Cob or Welsh Section D type; an excellent all-rounder.*

HIGHLAND PONIES

There is plenty of variety in this tough little breed. They are stocky animals with little ears, flowing manes and tails, and long hair around the feet. Their eyes are set well apart and they come in a wide range of colours, including chestnut with a silver mane and tail. They may show 'zebra-stripes' on the knees and hocks. Standing between 12.2–14.2 hands, the heavier representatives tend to be found on the Scottish mainland (they are called garrons) and the lighter ones on the Western Isles. They possess plenty of Arab and French pony blood.

DALES PONIES

Dales ponies originate from the northern counties of England and the neighbouring lowland areas of Scotland. They were important pack animals essential to commerce for hundreds of years right up until the nineteenth century. They stand up to 15 hands and are more massively built than Fell ponies. Their colour is mainly black, although not quite as much as in Fell ponies, and white markings are permissible.

FELL PONIES

Originating from the same general areas as Dales ponies, the Fells were essentially riding animals used on the uplands whereas the heavier Dales had their place in the valleys where industry and trade were centred. Fell ponies are mainly black with a small number of browns, bays and greys. They stand up to 14.2 hands and trot fast and tirelessly. The presence of foreign blood in their make-up (Friesian, Dolehest and Fjord pony) recalls the settlement of England's northern counties at various times in history by invaders from the Low Countries and Norway.

OPPOSITE TOP: *Dales ponies were originally used as pack animals for carrying loads of lead.*
OPPOSITE BOTTOM: *A Fell pony. These ponies came originally from the west of the Pennines whereas the Dale ponies came from the east of those hills.*
BELOW: *A fine grey Highland pony. The smaller Highlands are found on the Western Isles.*

COMMON AMERICAN BREEDS

After the mysterious disappearance of horses from the Americas in around 6000 BC, over seven thousand years passed before these animals were re-introduced by the Spanish colonists. Much credit for the conquistadors' success must be given to their four-legged companions, not least because of the way in which the appearance of these unknown 'monster' creatures instilled fear into the indigenous peoples confronted by the invaders. Thereafter, over the centuries, with the arrival of immigrants and their equines from every part of the world, different types of specifically American horses and ponies were developed by artificial selection. Some breeds are of relatively recent origin.

PONY OF THE AMERICAS

It was in 1954 that Les Boomhower, a breeder of Shetland ponies in Iowa, obtained an Arab/Appaloosa mare which had accidentally been mated with a Shetland stallion. When the foal was born it turned out to be a delightful little character with black smudges all over his body. Named Black Hand by Mr Boomhower, this was the first Pony of the Americas (POA). The new breed was quickly established, standards were set by the POA

BELOW: Around for less than fifty years, the Pony of the Americas is an attractive animal, perfect for beginners.

Club and the new ponies became a roaring success. They have a variety of coat patterns, the commonest being the so-called blanket pattern – white loins and limbs with dark round markings that can range in size from mere specks to patches of 10 cm/4 in or more in diameter. Some have spots all over the body – the leopard pattern.

Other characteristics are mottled skin (also found in the Appaloosa), a very visible white sclera (the white opaque part of the eyeball) and closely defined light or dark vertical stripes on the hooves (occasionally to be seen also in other breeds).

The POA is a gentle and easily trainable individual – intelligent, durable and of a steady temperament, it is the ideal pony for beginners.

OCRACOKE PONY (BANTER PONY)
Ocracoke Island off the North Carolina coast is home to a pony breed whose origins lie in a variety of romantic legends. Some say these ponies are the descendants of horses brought from Spain by Cortez as he searched for gold while exploring eastwards to Mexico. Others prefer a story of a ship carrying a circus and all its animals that sank in a storm, all perishing with the exception of two horses. Experts believe that the most probable ancestors of the breed were ponies brought with the Raleigh expeditions that were left on Roanoke Island at the time of the mysterious lost colony. These ponies, which are protected by the National Park Service, roam 65 hectares/160 acres of Ocracoke Island.

CHINCOTEAGUE PONY
Assateague Island, 60 km/37 miles long, lies off the coast of Maryland and Virginia. The ponies living there are feral animals – descendants of domesticated animals that have reverted to the wild. Where did they come from? Some say a shipwrecked Spanish galleon, but more probably they are descended from horses brought to the island in the seventeenth century by owners living on the mainland who were anxious to avoid livestock taxes.

The Chincoteague 'pony' may well be a 'horse' that averages only 12–13 hands in height due to the low-quality food supply and inclement environment. These ponies survive on coarse salt marsh grasses, twigs and seaweeds and drink very salty, brackish water.

Two main herds live on the island – one at the Maryland end, the other at the Virginia end. Each state manages its own herd and, by selling excess stock and administering contraceptive drugs by flying darts, keeps their numbers down to a maximum of 150 per herd.

AMERICAN WALKING PONY
This breed was developed in the 1960s from a foundation of Tennessee Walking Horse and Welsh Pony. From the former it inherited an elegant, smooth saddle gait; from the latter an exquisite head and long, arched neck. The various Walking Pony gaits are passed down from generation to generation and they include the delightfully named Pleasure Walk and the Merry Walk. Riding these ponies with their ability to move smoothly and change lightly from one gait to another is truly memorable.

QUARTER PONY
This popular, even-tempered pony is a mini Quarter Horse, developed from some of the latter which did not attain the American Quarter Horse Association's original minimum height requirement of 14.2 hands. Unlike its larger relative, it comes in a variety of colours.

On average, most Quarter Ponies are about 13.2 hands and are excellent for small riders, although bigger, heavily muscled ponies are now being raised. These powerful animals make fine mounts for large riders and can commonly be seen at country events, taking part in steer wrestling competitions ('bull dogging').

CAYUSE INDIAN PONY

Less well known than the POA, and nowadays found mostly in California, this small and steady pony with high withers and unusually long cannon bones, is probably a descendant of French horses brought to Canada in the seventeenth century. Later, Pawnee Indians crossed these European ponies with lighter-built Spanish Arabs, producing a tough, fast-running pony with unbounded stamina. By the early 1800s, as a result of careful selective breeding by the Cayuse Indians, the Cayuse Indian Pony was a separate breed, notable for its colourful coat with a tendency towards abundant white markings or spots.

BELOW: *The Cayuse Indian pony was developed by native Americans from European pony stock.*

OTHER PONY BREEDS

Across the world there are several hundred distinct breeds of pony – some in abundance, some extremely rare. As well as providing pure riding pleasure for folk of all ages, they may also be found carrying farmers and shepherds as they go about their work, as beasts of burden and pullers of wheeled vehicles, in specialist roles in the game of polo or the wild races of the Mongolian steppes and even, in some places, as providers of milk! Watch out for these breeds on your travels and ask the locals about them. Here are just a few.

BELOW: The tiny Falabella pony whose origins are most mysterious.

Avelignese: A pack pony from the Alps and Appenines of Italy.

Balearic: A rare working pony which you may be lucky enough to see in the orange groves of Majorca in the Balearic Islands.

Bashirsky: A pony breed from Russia whose mares produce milk which is drunk by folk for its medicinal properties. One mare can produce over 1818 litres (400 gallons) of milk during a 'milking season' of seven months.

Bosnian: A super-tough, intelligent, multi-purpose pony from Yugoslavia.

Camarguais: The famous grey-white pony of the marshes of France. It has one more lumbar vertebra (seven) than most other horses.

Dulmen: A disappearing breed from the Westphalian area of Germany.

Falabella: The smallest horse in the world, which stands under 70 cm/28 in high. It has to look up at a Great Dane! There are various fables as to how the breed originated from a strange dwarf horse that wandered out of the South American jungle years ago, but the facts seem to be that it is the result of selective inbreeding by the Falabella family of Recreo de Roca Ranch, near Buenos Aires, from the offspring of an original Shetland pony/thoroughbred cross. You can see these diminutive but hardy creatures at some stables and wildlife parks around the world.

Galiceno: A breed brought to Mexico from Spain by the explorer Cortes and now popular throughout the United States. It is gentle by nature and an excellent child's pony.

Garrano: The Portuguese pony, unchanged since the times of cavemen's drawings.

Haflinger: A mountain expert for the Austrian Tyrol, this pony is a strong worker up to an age of 35 years or more!

Manipur: The traditional breed in Assam. Polo was played on them as early as AD 625.

Marwari: The cavalry pony of the Mogul emperors of India.

Sable Island: A breed of only 200–300 ponies, descended from the eighteenth-century New England breeds. These ponies live with little shelter on the bleak, barren

Sable Island, off the coast of Nova Scotia.

🐎 **Sandalwood:** A fast racer which hails from the Indonesian lands of Sumbra al Sumbrawa.

🐎 **Senner:** A native German breed. Some are said to be living still truly wild in the forests around Bielefeld.

🐎 **Spiti:** A tough, high-altitude mountain climber from the Himalayas.

🐎 **Taishuh:** A strong, rugged pony from Japan, it dates back to the eighth century. Only about 70 individuals now exist.

🐎 **Vyatka:** A tough Russian pony in need of protection as its numbers are now no more than 2000. In the nineteenth century, this handsome pony was considered to be the best troika horse in Russia.

🐎 **Yonaguni:** Another rare pony which is native to the southwest islands of Japan. Usually chestnut in colour, gentle by nature and very strong, its ancestors arrived in the islands at about the time of Christ.

BELOW: *The Haflinger pony was bred for hard work in the mountains of the Austrian Tyrol.*

CHAPTER TWO

ACQUIRING YOUR PONY

Acquiring a good pony that is sound and of pleasing conformation is a potential minefield for the unwary. While the majority of pony vendors are honest and often knowledgeable, some unscrupulous horse dealers also lurk in the undergrowth. Of course, you may be giving a good home to a poor old moke rescued by some organisation, such as the Horses and Ponies Protection Association – if you are taking on such an animal, three cheers for you and you'll undoubtedly be well-rewarded. However, if you are purchasing the beast – beware. The world is full of pitfalls for the pony buyer and you need to follow the guidelines on the next few pages.

CHOOSING A PONY

Acquiring a pony should never be undertaken lightly. Before deciding to proceed and making your choice of animal, there are some important considerations to be taken into account by you and your family.

YOUR CIRCUMSTANCES

Do you have access to stabling and good or poor grazing? Do you have someone who can care for the pony while you're away on holiday?

A tough, native breed pony on good grazing with shelter will need less food than a more delicate 'blue-blood' pony on sparser grazing – up to 75 per cent less! It is more expensive to have a pony 'boarded out' at livery.

WHAT KIND OF PONY?

What sort of pony do you want and for what purposes? Native breeds are cheaper to keep, hardier and generally easier to handle than thoroughbred ones. Riding-school ponies are understandably more stoical and amenable by and large than privately owned (sometimes spoiled!) ones. Gelding ponies are somewhat more placid than mares.

WHAT SIZE OF PONY?

Young people grow faster than ponies. In general, a sturdy 14.2 pony will carry children and adults of most sizes but do try it out by sitting on it. The only rule is: does it feel right?

WHAT AGE OF PONY?

Not too young and inexperienced, not too old and fixed in its (possibly undesirable) ways. I believe a good age is seven to nine years. A pony that old is usually about to enter its best years and will steadily improve until it is approaching 20. Even after that, although perhaps with less vigour than before, the animal can give you at least 10 years or more. The better you keep the pony, the longer its active life. Very old ponies can be just the thing for the small or more nervous children.

LEFT: *It is vital to try out a pony for size and 'fit' by riding it before buying. Does it feel right for YOU?*

COST OF MAINTENANCE

Can you afford the costs of routine maintenance of a pony? As well as buying food (and perhaps grazing), stabling (or livery) fees, you must also budget for insurance, veterinary fees (hopefully your pony will remain healthy but even so there will be annual protective vaccination against tetanus and 'flu, and worming several times a year), the cost of tack and equipment, and hoof trimming and shoeing by the blacksmith between two and eight times a year.

WHERE TO OBTAIN YOUR PONY

You may be lucky enough to be offered a pony that you know well by a friend or your local riding school. Pony protection societies frequently look for good homes where they can place (loan rather than sell) their rescued animals. Then there are advertisements in the horsey magazines as well as pony dealers and pony auctions. When assessing a potential purchase, it is essential for you to get the guidance and good advice of someone with experience – a member of the pony club, your riding school, a blacksmith or another established pony owner. But besides that, whatever you do, before you part with any cash, have the pony 'vetted' by your veterinary surgeon, a process for which you will have to pay a fee but which will be money well spent.

WHAT SHOULD YOU EXPECT?

Firstly, you should look at the pony.
▲ Is it alert, bright, interested in you?
▲ Is it calm and amenable when approached and touched?
▲ Are its movements fluid and easy?
▲ How does it react to saddling up, to being ridden?
▲ Ride the pony yourself. Does it go

ABOVE: *Have the pony walked around so that you can assess its movement and temperament.*

smoothly and willingly or is it sluggish and awkward?
▲ Have it trotted away from and then towards you. Does it nod its head when one but not the other fore foot takes the weight? If so, it may indicate lameness. Is each hind foot placed equally firmly, and for the same length of time, on the ground – if not, again, there could be some lameness.
▲ Have the pony walked in a tight circle, while on a lead rein or halter, first clockwise and then anti-clockwise. Does it turn smoothly without stumbling? When backed up, does it do so without protest and free of any exaggerated action of the hind legs?
▲ If possible, see the pony out on the road. What is it like when close to traffic – skittish or as cool as a cucumber?

INSPECT THE PONY

The first rule is to make sure that you have the animal inspected thoroughly before you hand over any cash. Get someone who really knows horses, preferably your own veterinary surgeon, to overhaul the animal. Everything has got to be sound and in good working order, even if the conformation – the shape and make-up of the animal – may be imperfect, unpretty or unbalanced aesthetically in some respects. In a pet for the keen young rider, conformation and looks should not normally be of great concern, provided that any points of bad conformation do not represent areas of potentially weak anatomy. Horsey terms concerned with conformation include 'goose rump' (quarters that drop

RIGHT: *Check the pony's hooves for trapped stones, frog trouble and splits in the walls.*

EXAMINING THE PONY

Although the vet will carry out a detailed examination, you should try to check certain things yourself. Find out the answers to some questions. What is the pony's age? Is the conformation of the animal satisfactory? What is its height?

Run your hands over the body and legs. Are there any odd lumps or bumps or scars in the saddle area or on the limbs? Does the pony resent being touched anywhere? Pick up a foreleg and then a hind leg, handle the tail, moving it gently from side to side – is the pony happy to oblige? Do the hooves look in good condition? Check for signs of overgrowth of the hoof, uneven wear or horizontal ridges and grooves on the hoof wall that may indicate past bouts of laminitis. Is the frog of each foot well formed and the sole gently arched? Stand back and look at the pony's legs. Does each foreleg and each hind leg match the one on the other side?

In all of this, take your time. Don't rush to make a decision. Pay attention to your gut feelings – do you like the pony; does it like you; do you both 'click'?

steeply to the tail), 'toad eye' (prominent eyes) and 'cow hocks' (hocks that lean in towards one another). However, a little bit of any of these doesn't automatically mean that the pony is unsound or likely to be anything but a great deal of fit fun.

Some points of conformation are obviously undesirable because they probably signify trouble. For example, 'boxy feet' – steep, narrow, punched-in hooves – can be just asking for lameness, and a 'ewe neck', which,

like that of a shorn sheep, is concave on its upper edge, may suggest neck muscles that are not as flexible as they should be and so could cause schooling and balance problems.

RIGHT: *The correct position for checking the foreleg.*

ABOVE: *Regularly check the saddle area, looking for signs of rubbing, galls or abrasions.*

DETAILED EXAMINATION

The animal generally should be compact and neat, with a head in proportion to its body. When you are examining the pony, check the points that are listed here so that you are satisfied that its health and conformation are sound. Better still, as advised, get your vet or an expert to check the pony over for you.

Withers and back

Check for strange swellings on the withers and for saddle-produced sores or scars. The back must be neither arched ('roached') nor sunken, but straight and neither too long nor too short. The withers should be inconspicuous and the quarters should continue evenly the line of the back and then slope gracefully without sudden angling to the tail-head.

Coat

Check the health of the skin and hair, and its freedom from skin disease and parasites. Check all over the body for warts, wounds, bumps, lumps and other oddities.

Tail

Check the hair and for absence of disease or old injuries.

Hooves

All hooves should be well-formed and intact, with good soles and frogs (V-shaped pads on the soles): check the wall, sole and frog of each hoof for cleanliness and absence of disease.

Chest

The chest ought to be deep in relation to the distance between it and the ground, and the ribs well sprung. Check that the chest movements are smooth and unlaboured.

Eyes
These should be large and amiable. Check for normal anatomy and function. Any discharge? The vet may well look into each eye with an ophthalmascope.

Ears
Check for activity, good voluntary mobility and absence of discharge.

Neck
This should not be lean or scrawny.

Nostrils
These should be wide. Check for size and absence of discharge.

Mouth
Check the teeth for age (see page 40), alignment and condition of both the incisors and molars. Can they chomp up hay efficiently? The incisors should meet exactly. Check for gum disease and gum colour.

Legs
There should be four legs! Each foreleg must be so straight that a vertical line would run from the point of the shoulder down through the centre of the limb and its foot. A vertical line from the point of the buttocks should likewise bisect the hind leg and foot. Pasterns and hocks must not slope over-much. There should be no scars, abnormal swellings, tender areas, bumps or nobbles on any limb, and the feet should be turned neither inwards like a pigeon's nor out like a duck's. In a nutshell, the legs must be clean, neat, bold and strong.

The pony's chest

The vet will listen to the heart and lung sounds with a stethoscope. No coughing should be present; beware the tale, 'Oh, he's only coughing because I stirred up some dust in the stable when I opened a bale of hay five minutes ago'.

You can feel the heart beat with your hand and hear it by pressing your head against the pony's chest on the left side at the point of the elbow; the pulse is usually taken under one branch of the lower jaw. The heart rate of ponies at rest is about 45 beats per minute (newborn foals about 90 per minute). The rate gradually decreases throughout the first year of life. An occasional missed beat is not uncommon in healthy animals, but the vet will look for the cause. Breathing should be silent and regular when resting, with about 10–12 breaths per minute. This may increase to 80 or even 100 breaths per minute after intensive exertion.

After examining the chest at rest, the vet will want the pony exercised quickly for a short time to see what happens to the pulse and to hear the breathing rate. A fit animal rapidly returns to normal after a spell of exertion. Failure to do so may indicate lung or heart trouble.

Droppings

Check for consistency, colour, smell and general appearance. Is there any evidence of undigested food? There may be no obvious worms, but this can and must be confirmed, preferably before or at least as soon as possible after purchase, by asking the vet to do a microscopical examination of the droppings. This is very important in donkeys, which often carry lung-worms. If they are to be companions to ponies, check their droppings first for signs of lung-worms so they can receive regular worming if necessary and

thus avoid cross-infection. Ponies do pass wind from time to time. Excessive or very frequent flatulence may indicate indigestion. Ignore rumbling tummy noises to be heard in the abdominal area.

Urine

Check the colour. There is a variety of colours and consistencies of normal equine urine. Often perfectly healthy urine contains a white or creamy sludge. Black or obviously bloody urine needs immediate veterinary attention.

Demeanour

Is the animal alert, perky and interested in everything going on around him? He should not be listless and dull.

Movement

Does the pony move freely and easily without a stilted or abnormal gait? The vet will want to watch someone walk, trot and perhaps canter and gallop the pony. He or she will want to see it backed up and turned in tight clockwise and anti-clockwise circles. All or any of these movements may reveal lameness or faults in gait, balance or co-ordination. When walking or trotting up the pony, don't hold the halter rope too close to the head to give it plenty of rope. Look ahead of you as you lead it towards, across the front of or away from the vet. If it's for riding, see it saddled and harnessed. Check the fit of all the equipment – are there any points of pinching, rubbing or irritation?

Behaviour

Watch the animal's behaviour in its familiar environment. How does it feed? Are there any signs of vices – bad habits that can be difficult to eradicate and debilitating to the pony? The vet should pick up signs of these vices during the physical examination, but others are trickier to detect and may need time and observation of the animal's behaviour in its stable. Vices include 'crib-biting' (chewing anything within reach, particularly woodwork), 'wind-sucking' (swallowing air) and 'weaving' (a repetitive rocking from side to side). They tend to manifest themselves only in the stable, not when the animal is out at pasture.

FINALLY...

If you are finally satisfied and decide to buy your pony, try to get it on approval for as long as possible. Try also to get a warranty certifying full soundness, signed by a qualified vet. Make sure that you have any vaccination certificates relating to your pet. When you take it back to its new home, let it familiarize itself with its surroundings for a day or so before riding it. If you have other equines, don't mix them immediately – let them get to know each other for a day or two, separated by a stable half-door or a fence.

INSURANCE

Ponies are best insured against accidental death, veterinary fees, loss of use and third-party risks. Several insurance companies offer policies but premium rates and conditions vary so check and compare first.

Sadly ponies are sometimes stolen, principally for the horse meat trade on the European continent. A powerful deterrent to such thefts is freeze-branding. This entails putting a permanent number on the animal's skin by way of an iron cooled in liquid nitrogen. This method of branding is completely humane and is available from a number of companies advertising in horsey journals.

BELOW: *These two friends are enjoying themselves in the summer sunshine. Pony ownership confers certain responsibilities but it's well worth it.*

AGEING

Telling the age of a pony can be easier in some cases than others. It is not an exact science and is more prone to error at certain ages. Like some second-hand car dealers, unscrupulous sellers of horse-flesh can attempt to 'doctor' the age of their wares, even by actually tampering with the physical appearance of the animal's teeth. However, what is tolerated in the case of lady film stars, actresses and the like – the majority of whom suspend the laws of time at round about the age of twenty-one years – is definitely not permissible when you, the innocent purchaser, are looking for a long-eared and four-footed friend.

There is nothing wrong as such with a pony that has passed middle age or even trotted into its dotage, but you need to know more or less accurately how long it is in the tooth. Actually it is not just the length of the teeth, but certainly the information needed for ageing your pet is all to be found in its dentures. So what are horsey folk doing when they grab a mean hold on their mount's tongue (not at all a painful procedure although it looks most undignified) and stare, nodding wisely, into the horse's mouth? They are looking at certain features of the teeth – numbers, types, shapes, marks – all of which give clues (accurate up to eight years and somewhat less so up to about 30 years of age) as to how many birthdays their equine has seen. The technique is the same in horses, ponies and donkeys.

TEETH

Ponies generally have 42 teeth, composed of:
- Twelve incisors (front teeth)
- Four tushes (canine or fang teeth)
- Twenty-four cheek teeth (molars)
- Two rudimentary molars called 'wolf teeth'.

Both 'milk' and permanent sets of incisors and cheek teeth are to be found in the pony and donkey, but tushes and wolf teeth (when present) are permanent only. 'Milk' teeth are somewhat triangular, shell-like and lighter coloured than the more oblong, yellower, heavier-built permanent

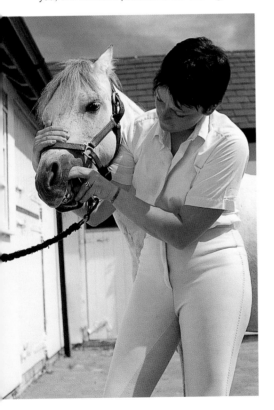

LEFT: The correct way of inspecting a pony's teeth in order to try and assess its age.

teeth. Mares rarely grow their tushes and often ponies don't produce wolf teeth either.

In Britain, it is traditional to take 1 May as the 'official birthday' of all equines – that is the base point from which tooth checks are judged. For ageing, we can ignore the developments in the cheek teeth and concentrate solely on the incisors, whose positions in each jaw are termed: central, lateral and corner.

How the teeth change

At birth, the foal has two central 'milk' incisors in upper and lower jaw.

At one month, the lateral incisors appear but don't meet their opposite numbers until five months. At this time, the corner incisors can be felt preparing to poke through the gums.

At one year, the corner incisors are well through but don't touch their fellows in the opposite jaw until one-and-a-half years.

At two years, all six upper incisors are perfectly aligned and touching the lower six. The central 'milk' incisors are beginning to get ideas of dropping out and are loosened from the gum edge.

At two-and-a-half years, the permanent central incisors push out their milk predecessors but don't meet.

At three years, they do.

At three-and-a-half years, the permanent laterals are through but not meeting. Tushes may appear in the males about now.

At four years, the permanent laterals meet.

At four-and-a-half years, the permanent corner teeth arrive on the scene.

At five years, all permanent incisors are through and meeting with the corners just so. Also at five years, the incisors possess in their wearing surfaces distinct dark hollows called 'marks'.

At six years, each incisor shows a smooth ring of worn tooth around its mark. The marks on the central incisors begin to fade in their intensity.

At seven years, the central and lateral marks are smaller, shallower and paler than on the corner teeth. A 'hook' develops on the upper corner teeth.

At eight years, the marks on all the teeth are faint and shallow. The 'hook' has almost or completely gone.

At nine years, a groove, Galvayne's groove, first appears on the upper corner incisor teeth. It steadily moves down the teeth and is halfway down at 15, fully down at 20, halfway out (only present in the lower half of the tooth) at 25 and is gone by 30 years. The length and position of Galvayne's groove is your best guide in the years between nine and 30, although experts also note changes in the tooth tables (wearing surfaces) and the angle of the teeth. Basically, as the years progress, the shape of the tooth tables change. Also, whereas, say, lower incisors are fairly upright chaps at 10 years of age, projecting at an angle of around 45 degrees above the horizontal, by the age of 30 they are leaning outwards at only 25 degrees.

ON SAFARI

Wild asses and zebras can be aged in the same way as ponies, but zebras go through the various stages roughly six months ahead of their domesticated cousins. I do not recommend that you try grabbing a zebra's tongue in order to practise your ageing skills when next you visit the local zoo or go on safari in Kenya.

CHAPTER THREE

FEEDING AND DIET

The correct feeding of your pony is much more than the provision of calories to fuel the riding and other activities of the animal. Tip-top health, good condition and smart appearance, as well as the steady growth and development of younger ponies, vitally depend upon it. No less than other fuel costs in the modern world, that of the pony continues to rise. The fuelling of our long-eared friends cannot be done on the cheap and demands constant, careful attention. As well as the right quantities of various foodstuffs, the pony's well-being depends on being fed only nutrients of the highest quality.

THE PONY'S NATURAL DIET

The ancestors of the pony were incredibly hardy beasts, and today its closest living wild relatives survive in some of the most inhospitable regions of the world where food is generally low in both quantity and quality. The Przewalski horse, which at usually less than 14 hands in height should really be classified as a pony, hails from the high steppes of Mongolia and Dzungaria, rocky arid, country bordering the Gobi Desert which is dry and hot in summer and bitterly cold in winter. The Przewalskis wander in search of tussock grass, tamarisk, wormwood and saxaul shrubs, which, though dry-looking, possess a juicy bark which the animals strip. They might go three or four days without water and in summer dig holes in the soil with their hooves, searching for a little salty water.

Kiangs come across good feed during only two months of the year, August and September, and have learnt to cope with the harsh swamp grass that is packed with silica and would cut the more sensitive mouths of their domesticated cousins to pieces. In January and February, they get their water requirements by eating snow, apparently without harm. Onagers root around in the deserts for any grasses or plants that can grow in the scorched and barren wilderness. They survive by cropping over 100 varieties of edible plants, which absorb moisture from the atmosphere during the cool nights, and by scoffing a fair quantity of the salty soil of their environment. African wild asses, denizens of regions where the temperature may reach 50°C (122°F), need to do plenty of grazing in order to fill their stomachs from the lean pickings of the parched, rocky landscape. They are up early, foraging at daybreak, then lying up in the heat of the day, and feeding again from around 5 pm until sunset.

Happily, our domesticated ponies don't have to put up with that sort of life. Today's pony feeds well and healthily and should know nothing of hunger, thirst and hard times. However, in Britain, as elsewhere, the cost of animal foodstuffs rises steadily in the face of ever-growing demand from meat and grain eating human populations.

OPPOSITE: Ponies doing what comes naturally. This pair will be fully nourished by a pasture plainly in excellent condition.

THE IDEAL DIET

The quantity and make-up of your pony's ration will depend on the following:

🐎 Whether or not it is grazing

🐎 Its size and body weight

🐎 The amount of work it does.

Adjustment of each particular ration is necessary after experience has shown whether or not an animal 'does well' on what it is given. Some individuals need a little more concentrated food than others in order to stay perky and in spanking good condition; other ponies need a little less to prevent them becoming too stroppy and fiery.

Under ideal natural conditions, a pony would obtain all the nutrients it needs from the variety of plant-life in the pastures on which it grazes. 'Grass' in such a case is far more than the green stubbly stuff that Dad mows on a Sunday afternoon; indeed, it is a remarkable variety of vegetation containing weeds, seeds, flowers, shoots, stems, leaves and bits of soil that contribute the necessary carbohydrates, protein, fats, minerals and vitamins. Over 150 different sorts of wild grass alone grow in Britain. However, most of our ponies are not kept on ideal pasture, or they graze for only part of the year. Many are kept in paddocks where there is little either in quality or quantity of plant growth. Others are stabled permanently.

Important: For information on poisonous types of vegetation, see page 59.

BELOW: *This pony is in tip-top condition. Health and condition vitally depend on correct feeding.*

BULK FOODS

🔺 **Hay:** There are many varieties of hay and it is important to obtain and feed good-quality stuff which is more nutritious and won't make your pet poorly. Hay that hasn't 'cured' correctly after cutting can cause lung and kidney irritation as well as tummy upsets. Good hay smells like a new-mown meadow, contains leaves of a pale pastel green and has flower-heads still attached to the stalks. Hay that is crumbly and smells musty, or is damp and sour in parts of the bale, or is very dusty, or is obviously affected here and there with whitish mould, or is dark brown and smells like tobacco, should be rejected.

🔺 **Chaff:** Also known as 'cavings'. This can be either chopped hay or straw. It is an excellent fibrous, bulk-providing foodstuff, which is better balanced than bran and much to be preferred to the latter.

🔺 **Bran:** This is a traditional 'horsey' dish, although it isn't very much liked by our equine friends, and nowadays, because modern milling methods have removed the flour it once contained, it has little food value. Its mineral content is not well balanced: there is too much phosphorus and not enough calcium in most samples of bran. Feeding an excessive amount of bran can lead to bone diseases, such as Big Head or Miller's Disease. Nevertheless, it does provide fibrous bulk and therefore can be used for its mild laxative effect, made up as a mash (see box).

🔺 **Root vegetables:** Carrots, turnips and sugar beet provide bulk, sugars and vitamins. They must, however, be clean and free of rotten parts. Chop them up before serving. Sugar beet pulp must never be fed dry; it will swell up in the pony's innards and can cause colic, choking and even death. The pulp must always be soaked in water for at least six hours before feeding.

BRAN MASH

1 kg/2 lb bran

15 g/¹⁄₂ oz salt

900 ml/1¹⁄₂ pints boiling water

Mix well together and cover with a plate or thick cloth pressed well down onto the mash. Leave for 30 minutes and then feed when cool enough. To increase its appeal to ponies that usually regard it in rather the way that a diner at an expensive restaurant would cast his eye over an unsolicited bowl of cold porridge, add a couple of tablespoons of syrup, molasses or oats. Bran mash quickly goes sour, so always use it freshly made.

ENERGY-PRODUCING FEEDS

These feeds provide the rich food that is necessary for a pony that does work, in the winter and at other times when grazing is greatly reduced or absent.

🔺 **Oats:** The best-known energy food for equines is, of course, oats. The richness in calories of this sort of grain is accepted in common parlance; its ability to produce friskiness has led to phrases such as 'he cannot carry his corn' for someone who becomes less restrained after reaching prosperity, and 'he's feeling his oats' for a lively individual. Whole oats should be pleasant-smelling, dry, light in colour and free from dust. Mouldy oats smell 'off', produce dust or are faintly damp and can produce illnesses, ranging from chest trouble to kidney disease. Crushed and rolled oats are produced from whole oats by machinery which breaks the outer husk of the oats. The idea is to allow digestive juices more ready access to the nourishing, carbohydrate-rich interior. However, a normal pony can grind whole oats perfectly satisfactorily, and there can be difficulty in spotting sub-standard samples of oats after they have been broken by the machinery. All the same, I tend to prefer crushed oats and would advise, if possible, that you check the quality of some whole oats before buying and then get the miller to process the batch that you have selected. Crushed and rolled oats are particularly suitable for older animals, invalids and beasts with imperfect teeth.

FIBRE

All energy foods need to be fed along with fibre-containing or bulk foods in order to be sure that they are properly digested. The tummy of the pony is specially designed to do the job of breaking down the tough cellulose walls that surround the inner, nutritious parts of plant material. Whereas cattle, sheep, giraffes and other cud-chewing animals do this by means of an internal population of friendly digesting bacteria stored in four stomachs, our equine chums store the bacteria in greatly enlarged intestines. To function properly, these cavernous organs need plenty of fibre for the worker bacteria to perch on while working and to stimulate gentle contractions of the intestine wall.

Pony cubes and horse nuts: These 'compounded' foods are actually mixtures in pellet form made from dried grass, hay and grains with the addition of minerals and vitamins. They are carefully made to strict specifications and can form a complete diet. Their advantages are simplicity, scientific balance, freedom from dustiness and ease of storage. Their disadvantages are cost and low-roughage content. Animals fed nothing but nuts or cubes tend to root for roughage, and this may range from eating their bedding to slowly demolishing their surroundings by chomping at any available woodwork. Coarse mixes ('sweetfeeds' in the United States) are compressed feeds that are flaked rather than ground and cubed. Other energy foods are peas, beans and flaked maize. Grains such as barley and wheat should be avoided as they can induce colic.

SPECIAL FOODS

Chopped grass or lawn mowings: Although there is no doubt that cut green grass is perfectly as appropriate for ponies as if they had cropped it themselves, it must be fresh and fed in only small amounts. Once cut, grass soon starts to ferment and heat up, especially if it is very succulent and full of juice. In a pile, such heated grass rapidly decomposes and produces chemicals that can cause dangerous problems once inside your pet. Lawn mowings, being fine and tending to compress into a dense heap, ferment and heat more vigorously than grass cut with shears or a sickle and so present the greatest danger. If you feed mowings, do so very sparingly and only when just newly cut. If you have any doubts, DON'T give them, especially if chemicals, fertilizers or weedkillers have

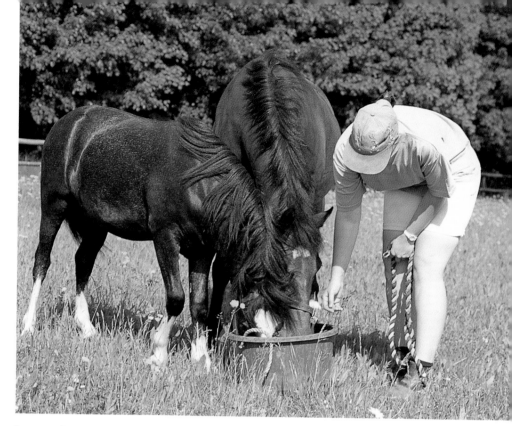

ABOVE: This couple are obviously keen to sample something other than grass.

been used on the lawn. Lucerne (alfalfa) is an excellent, nutritious foodstuff but should be given in moderate amounts.

Linseed: This is another energy source and traditionally used to impart a sleek and glossy condition to the coat. On no account must it be fed raw – it can induce violent colic – nor should it be soaked in cold or tepid water to make a 'mash' or it will release the highly poisonous chemical, prussic acid. Properly prepared by being boiled for three to four hours until it is a sticky porridge, allowed to cool and then fed, linseed mash is an excellent item on the winter menu.

Invalid foods: Gruels of oatmeal or barley meal are sometimes given to debilitated or convalescent animals. They are made by bringing 450 g/1 lb of meal to the boil in 4 litres/1 gallon of water and simmering for 20–30 minutes. The cooked gruel is allowed to cool and fed, usually with the addition of some more cold water. Many people don't realise that both eggs and milk are suitable invalid foods for ponies. Milk can be given in quantities of up to 2.5–3 litres/4–5 pints a day and at first will be found more palatable by the patient if watered down and very highly salted. Eggs (two to six) are given raw, either beaten up in milk or mixed with a mash.

Minerals and vitamins: Although your pet should get enough minerals and vitamins from grass and/or the other ingredients of its balanced diet, it's wise to play safe, especially in winter. Add the recommended quantity of one of the equine mineral/vitamin supplements (some with protein added) which you can buy from pet stores, food merchants and tack shops. These can be liquids, powders or large blocks. Salt blocks are a sensible item in the stable, and glucose blocks can be given as a sort of lollipop treat in the winter.

AMOUNTS OF FOOD

The right amount of food for the pony varies, depending on the weight and size of the animal, the work it does, the season of the year and the amount of grazing available. As with human beings, some ponies easily put on 'spare tyres', whereas others can gobble away and stay on the skinny side. Ponies at grass and doing a little light work need only a small quantity of energy food – the bulk comes from the pasture – and in spring, when the grass is rich in protein, the protein content of the energy food can be reduced.

The same ponies when stabled must be given both the bulk food and a higher quantity of energy food. Some ponies become rather 'fresh', stroppy and unruly on too high a proportion of energy food and will need it cutting down: too rich a fuel makes their engines 'pink', but then four-star petrol ain't right for two-star engines! Others, the sluggish, dreamy types, may benefit from having it increased.

Sometimes, cutting the oats down to reduce stroppiness is accompanied by a loss of weight. In this case, substitute linseed mash or flaked maize for the oats. Ponies that have a good temperament but tend to run to fat should have their hay reduced.

It's all a question of adjusting the diet composition and amounts to the particular

WATER

Domesticated ponies must be provided with plenty of clean, fresh water. They will consume between 9.5–19 litres/2–4 gallons every day. If there is no constant supply, give the water in buckets before feeding, not after. A hot, bothered pony that has just returned from vigorous exercise should be rested and cooled and have the sweat removed before watering.

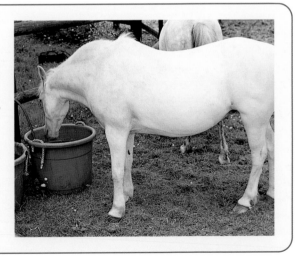

TYPICAL FEEDING PROGRAMMES

Pony size	Routine	Summer diet	Winter diet
14.2 hands	Out at grass during the day. Stabled at night. Ridden every day plus schooling, shows, etc.	Grass during day. 3 kg/1½ lb hay and 3-4 kg/1½-2 lb pony nuts and a handful of carrots.	5-7 kg/11-15 lb hay and 4-5 kg/9-11 lb pony nuts and some carrots.
14.0 hands	Out at grass during the day all year. Stabled at night in winter. Ridden every day in summer, twice weekly in winter.	Grass during day and 2 kg/4 lb pony nuts if necessary.	5-7 kg/11-15 lb hay and 2.5-3.5 kg/5-7 lb pony nuts and a handful of carrots.
13.0 hands	Out at grass all year. Ridden daily in summer but only at weekends in winter.	Grass only.	6 kg/13 lb hay and 1-1.5 kg/2-3 lb pony nuts and a handful of carrots.

requirements of your pet. It won't take you long to get the feel of it. Fiddling about with the diet and watching the effect won't do him a scrap of harm. Above is a table for feeding ponies of different sizes with varying routines in summer and winter to give you some general guidance in the early days of keeping your new pony.

If you decide to feed 'complete' horse and pony cubes that contain a lot of fibre and don't need hay in addition, then follow the manufacturers' recommendations on the bag for daily quantities.

SPECIAL CONDITIONS

If a pony is kept outside throughout the winter, it is an excellent idea to give him warm feeds of linseed mash every other day during foul weather in addition to the regular diet. Ponies kept under these conditions are best provided with hay ad lib.

If your pony is about to enter a period of increased activity (the summer season of

shows, holidays, etc.), increase the energy food accordingly. If he is ill or lame and 'off the road', reduce the energy food, give a little extra hay and use some bran mash to keep the bowels in order.

Whenever you change the diet, do it gradually. Finally, the golden rule: feed little and often. Four feeds a day are better than two, and two are better than one.

FOOD FOR HEALTH

Good feeding contributes much to good skin health. An occasional linseed mash will help to give the coat a sheen and, in dry-skinned individuals, an occasional course of unsaturated fatty-acid in powder form added to the food is very beneficial. This type of product can be obtained from a veterinary surgeon, pet shop or tack shop.

CHAPTER FOUR

HOUSING AND GENERAL CARE

Wherever your pony lives, its year-round accommodation will depend on several factors. The kind of pony he is, the climate in your area, the quantity and quality of grazing available and what kind of shelter from the elements is in place must all be taken into consideration. You may choose to stable your pony indoors, to keep him out at grass or to do a bit of both. You must decide which method suits you and, more importantly, the pony best.

AT GRASS

If you have got a piece of land for your pet, it cannot be regarded as permanent grazing unless it's at least 0.9 hectare/2 acres in size – and by that I mean good green stuff, not a rocky desert or a converted bomb-site! A good rule is to calculate a minimum of 1 hectare/$2^1/2$ acres per pony, but even so the land will need 'resting' for a month or two each year and will need not only its own grooming in the form of attention to weeds, such as nettles, docks and the dangerous ragwort, which can cause liver disease in equines, but also fertilization with lime or other chemicals, depending on the soil. After spraying weedkillers and certain fertilizers, the animal must be kept off the ground for a period that can be as long as two or three weeks in the case of some brushwood killers (carefully read the instructions that come with the preparation you use).

It helps the land to graze more than one species together – for example, ponies with sheep and cattle. They reduce one another's parasites and one species trims back types of plants that the other ignores. Obviously, however, the more animals of any species, the more land they require.

If the pasture is large enough, try some form of rotational grazing, splitting it up with light fencing or electric fencing into zones that can be grazed and then rested in turn. Where you are really pushed for land, daily removal of the pony's droppings by a bucket and shovel will help to keep the grass clear and reduce the worm burden. Remember that some ponies tend to founder on fresh grass when it first comes in during spring.

BELOW: *This contented pair are grazing on obviously good quality and abundant grass.*

FENCING AND GATES

This is expensive and you may have to put up with whatever comes with the land you rent or buy. Inspect your fencing regularly and keep it well maintained. At all costs, try to avoid barbed wire as a fencing material. It is vicious stuff!

ABOVE: *Protect young trees from ponies by erecting some protective fencing around them.*

ABOVE: *If you use electric fencing to split up a field for grazing, remember to clearly mark it.*

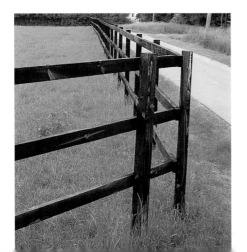

LEFT: *Stout three bar fencing with the fence posts on the 'outside' of the field is expensive but ideal. You must regularly maintain the fence, repairing any broken sections quickly and weather-proofing the timber.*

RIGHT: *Temporary wire mesh fencing is cheap and easy to handle but dangerous to ponies who can easily break it down and trap their legs in the holes. If you must use it, for example, to keep grazing animals out of newly planted areas, create a barrier between it and your ponies with electric fencing which is suitably marked.*

ABOVE: *A strong wooden gate, with strong hinges, which opens into the field is recommended. Heavy metal gates can rust easily, be difficult to open while handling ponies and can trap a pony's hoof in the grid. Note the white electric strip along the fence to protect the saplings.*
RIGHT: *A metal sprung gate handle, which requires only one hand to open and close the gate, is ideal.*

ABOVE: *Remember to padlock a remote or isolated field to prevent other people accidentally leaving the gate open and for your animal's security.*

FIELD SHELTERS

Even if you have enough land to keep your pet out of doors, it still needs shelter from the elements, particularly in winter. An open shed or shelter, one that has the front partly closed, is essential. It should be big enough to give

ABOVE: It is important to select the best position for a field shelter, preferably on dry, well-drained soil with the entrance facing away from prevailing winds.

BELOW: Field shelters are best constructed of creosoted wood, bricks or breeze blocks. Corrugated iron is fine for roofs but best not used for walls. It is a

WATER SUPPLY

Plastic dustbins make good water containers for ponies. They are not knocked over as easily as buckets and don't clip the pony's knees as old metal baths are prone to do.

poor insulator and easily works loose or curls at the edges. The result can be annoying rattling or, even worse, injuries to the animals.

HOW TO TELL IF YOUR PONY IS COLD

If a pony feels cold, it may or may not shiver and tend to be reluctant to move away from any available shelter. Place the flat of your hand on its skin over the chest and flanks; if the surface is uniformly cold it is best to warm the animal up straight away by vigorous grooming ('strapping') or, particularly when wet, rubbing down with a twist of straw ('wisping'), bringing indoors to the shelter or stable and/or rugging it.

A sensitive pony exposed to much cold, particularly if wet as well, may develop respiratory problems.

ABOVE: *Although many tough native ponies do not need rugging in winter, more delicate types and 'senior citizens' appreciate the comfort of a New Zealand rug worn continuously in cold weather.*

one animal about 11 m^2/120 ft^2 with an extra 5 m^2/50 ft^2 for every additional animal. It need not be anything fancy so long as the roof does not leak and the walls are intact. The floor, which may be plain earth, must be dry and spread with straw in winter. The only equipment required is a supply of fresh, clean water and maybe a hay net.

There is no need to remove soiled bedding from the shelter. Just regularly scatter clean new straw on top, thereby gradually building up a comfortable 'deep litter' bed.

Nor is there any need for a door on the shelter. Ponies prefer the entrance left open – so they can see what's going on outside.

POISONOUS VEGETATION

Before putting a pony out to grass, or if you know the field where hay will be made for winter feeding for your animal, check for poisonous plants and don't forget to watch out for poisonous bushes and trees that may overhang from adjoining property. Some dangerous plants will only be eaten by ponies when other food is in short supply, or when they are dead and dried. Some have to be eaten regularly over weeks or months to cause their ill effects; others can kill after only a mouthful. Here are some of the most important toxic plants.

Yew *(Taxus spp.)*
Commonly found in English churchyards, this is deadly for equines. A handful can lead to fatal effects within minutes.

Bracken *(Pteridium aquilinum)*
Ponies usually only fancy bracken in late autumn or when other grub is scarce. It contains a chemical that destroys Vitamin B1. It usually has to be eaten over a period of months before producing symptoms.

Horsetail – also known as Marestail *(Equisetum spp.)*
Its effects are similar to those of bracken. It is usually eaten in hay.

Ragwort *(Senecio spp.)*
This causes liver damage after being consumed, usually in hay or when there is a shortage of other herbage, over weeks or months.
Note: Similar effects to Ragwort are produced by Rattleweed *(Crotalaria spp.)*, Peterson's Curse or Salvation Jane *(Echium spp.)* and Fiddleneck or Tarweed *(Amsinckia spp.)*.

Water Hemlock *(Cicuta spp.)* **and Hemlock** *(Conium maculatum)*
The symptoms of nervous system poisoning appear within two hours of ingestion.

Loco Weed *(Astragalus and Oxytropus spp.)*
Poisoning is commonest in spring on the ranges in the western United States.

Sneezeweed *(Helenium spp.)*
A common poisonous weed of damp fields in the eastern United States. The flowers are the most toxic part of the plant.

Yellow Star Thistle *(Centaurea sostitialis)*
This is found mainly in the United States. It has to be ingested in large amounts over an extended period.

White Snakeroot *(Eupatorium rugosum)*
This is found in the southern United States. The poison attacks the nervous system and can kill an animal within days.

Milkweed *(Ascelpia spp.)*, **Rhododendron** *(Rhododendron spp.)*, **and Foxglove** *(Digitalis spp.)*
All contain chemicals that affect the heart and can cause sudden death.
Note: There are many other poisonous plants that less frequently cause trouble for ponies; if you are in doubt as to the identity and safety of any plant that might be nibbled by your pet, take a specimen to your veterinary surgeon for identification.

SPRING GRASS

Many ponies are prone to founder on the lush, fresh grass when it first appears in spring. Ponies that tend to fatten easily need to be taken off this grass and either stabled or allowed to graze sparingly for only a few hours a day.

STABLING YOUR PONY

If you are stabling your pony indoors, you have the choice between a stalling system and a loose-box. The latter is preferable as it allows more space and freedom to move around. It should provide the same area as mentioned earlier for sheds on pasture, and should be dry and well-insulated. The floor should be non-slip (but not made of wood) and slightly sloping for easy drainage. It should be well-ventilated and provided both with windows, barred on the inside, and with electric light. There should be a two-part door at least 1.2 m/4 ft wide and opening outwards. There should be no sharp projections, latches or electric switches on the inside surfaces of the stable. If you use paint on the stable, never use lead-based paints.

MAINTENANCE

Somewhere near the loose-box should be a separate room where all the mucking-out implements, food, bedding and harness can be neatly stored. Food should be kept in galvanized, rodent-proof bins, and hay should also be held in well-built places where rat and mouse contamination is minimal. You will also need a suitable place for a muck-heap, and keeping a wheelbarrow.

Keep drains clear, walls, floors and windows clean, and tack and food stores, as well as

BELOW: *The door is the right height for this pony who will spend a lot of time looking out.*

BELOW: *A clean and tidy tack room is part of good pony-keeping practice.*

the stable, tidy at all times. You should keep your muck heap compact and tidy too – the more compact the muck is, the more it heats up and destroys worm eggs. To kill parasites in the cooler parts of the heap, turn them in with a fork occasionally.

You will also need clothing for your pet – a waterproof New Zealand rug, a stable rug with a roller to keep it on, a blanket or two and some bandages to protect legs and tails. These are basic requirements; show ponies need extra, special bits of togging.

Finally, proper fire precautions should be observed. Extinguishers should be placed in readily accessible spots close to the stables and the hay and food stores.

EQUIPMENT

Only basic equipment should be fitted in the stable. This comprises:

- ▲ A ring for tying up to when necessary
- ▲ A manger or trough
- ▲ A water-trough or bucket
- ▲ A hay net (optional).

STABLE COMPANIONS

Ponies are best stabled with a companion – another pony or a donkey that they get along with or, if no other equine is available, a sheep or a goat will fit the bill.

BELOW: *Whether you use straw, wood shavings or peat as bedding for your pony, you must always make sure that you have the correct facilities and equipment to correctly muck out the stable.*

MUCKING OUT

An essential daily job for the pony owner is mucking out the stable. An act of basic hygiene, it helps control the risk of certain ailments and it keeps the pony's living quarters dry and comfortable. Done correctly, using the right implements, it can take no more than a few minutes. And it is not really messy or smelly.

You will need a wheelbarrow, a shovel or long-handled scoop, a stout yard brush and a stable fork. It is best to turn the pony out and remove any portable water containers while mucking out.

1 Using the fork or shovel, put all dung and wet and dirty bedding into the wheelbarrow and take it to the muck heap, which should be situated well away from the stables.

2 Fork the rest of the bedding away from the centre of the floor so that it lies against the walls of the stable.

3 Use a stout brush to sweep the floor so that it is ready for the new bedding.

DEEP LITTER SYSTEM

Alternatively, you can turn over the bedding by fork each day so that the droppings are buried. Very wet patches should be removed, and damp patches covered by dry bedding. A little clean bedding is now scattered all over. Gradually the layer of bedding builds up and its lower levels begin to produce heat by fermentation, killing parasites and other bugs, absorbing any damp and generally creating a warm, snug bed for the pony. Whereas traditional mucking out requires 3–6 bales of straw for one week, deep litter can be maintained on one or less. After some months, perhaps as long as a year, when it is becoming difficult for you to get into the stable, remove the bed and start again.

BEDDING DOWN

Stable bedding should be deep enough so that when a fork is stuck into it, the prongs do not touch the floor. Build up the bedding around the sides of the stable to keep out draughts, protect the pony from abrasions when lying down against a wall and prevent it becoming wedged when lying down and then unable to rise.

Some ponies love to eat their straw bedding and others are allergic to fungal spores in the straw which can cause coughing. For them, wood shavings, chopped hemp, dust-extracted straw or shredded paper are better bedding materials, but these are all more expensive than straw.

1 Using a fork or shovel, pile the straw up against a wall. Once a week disinfect the floor and leave it to air and dry for an hour or two before replacing the bedding.

2 Add new bedding, scattering it evenly in the centre of the stable.

3 Bank the bedding up against the walls, making it deeper around the sides.

4 Let your pony back into the stable and keep an eye on him until you are happy.

STABLE ROUTINE

A pony is not usually kept in its stable night and day – unless the weather is particularly bad or the animal is off colour, or there are other pressing reasons for doing so temporarily. Ponies thrive on space; they need to be able to stretch their legs, roll around when they feel inclined and generally exercise themselves in the open air. A pony housed indoors permanently can become irritable, fractious and prone to leg swelling and digestive upsets. Stabling at night and putting the pony out during the day is a good routine to get into. At the very least, a stabled pony should always have two hours outside, either being ridden or wandering free in a field or paddock, each day.

DAILY TIMETABLE

Assuming that you follow the 'in stable by night – in field by day' routine for your pet, there should be at least four feeds per day provided. Unlike some other species, ponies have digestive systems that do not function well on just morning and evening feeds. An ideal daily timetable is the following:

Early morning: Check the pony. Provide fresh water. Give first feed plus some hay.
Mid morning: Muck out stable. Basic light grooming. Exercise for 1-2 hours.
Around midday: Feed and give a full grooming. Provide more hay.
Afternoon: Pony free to wander in field or paddock.
Early evening: Feed, plus more hay. Put on night rug. Check bedding.
Last thing: Feed, plus more hay.

On any day when the pony has less than the usual amount of exercise, increase the amount of hay in the feeds and reduce the concentrates.

ABOVE: *Displaying obvious elation, ponies dash off when first turned out.*

GROOMING

The hairy coat of a pony is more than just an adornment and it does require regular attention and grooming from a thoughtful and proud owner. Obviously, wild ponies and asses don't get groomed – you would be lucky to get anywhere near them with a curry comb! But they do keep their coats in tip-top shape by mutual grooming and do-it-yourself mud-packs.

Wild ponies display elaborate grooming procedures which, apart from cleaning the coat, getting rid or parasites and generally tidying up loose hairs, also act as vital bits of socializing that keep the members of the herd committed to one another. Flicking of the skin caused by rapid contractions of subcutaneous muscles, shaking the body, licking and rubbing are all natural grooming movements. Scratching one hind leg against the other is never seen in wild ponies and horses but it is common among zebras.

Rolling in dust and mud is another favourite form of self-care for their upholstery, and experiments have shown that zebras will only 'recognise' and make overtures to a stuffed dummy zebra if it is first properly smeared with a generous helping of glorious mud!

The most important and highly developed form of skin care in equines is biting. They bite themselves but prefer to do it to one another. One animal approaches its fellows and puts on the so-called 'invitation face' (mouth closed and upper lip pulled forward). Without more ado they stand side by side, head to tail, nibbling away at one another's hide, rooting out old hairs, stimulating the blood flow and toning up the bodywork. Each animal bites at the

BELOW: *Ponies love being groomed – either by one another, OR BY YOU.*

same area of skin as the other. This behaviour is particularly important when winter coats begin to be shed and it is most prevalent during the summer. The moulting of a pony's coat is stimulated by the spring rise in air temperatures. In the last wild horse, the Przewalski, which should strictly be called a pony, the temperature at which moulting is triggered is 6°C/42°F.

This self-grooming in wild equines is all very well, but our domesticated chums need some regular and thorough help from their owner-drivers if they are to feel and look really good. Groom your pet properly and you will reduce the risk of skin disease, improve his condition and make him elegantly glossy.

GROOMING YOUR PONY

Whereas the fond car owner appears on the driveway with hose and polish most Sunday mornings or, more lazily, takes his steed down to the local car wash, pony owners must tend

LEFT: *This little character needs to have all the winter's mud brushed out of his coat.*

the appearance of their animals more regularly and frequently than that. Grooming is not a cosmetic procedure. Cleaning and brushing the coat has the following functions:

▲ It reduces the risk of skin disease

▲ Very importantly, it pleases the animal and strengthens the bond between rider and ridden

▲ It allows the groom to spot any minor cuts and injuries on the pony

▲ It stimulates the pony's circulation and muscle tone.

Ponies at grass in winter need little attention apart from a general looking-over once a week to remove any caked mud with a dandy brush, untangling of manes and tails, picking out and oiling of the hooves with neat's foot or some proprietary hoof oil, and a general brushing-down of the coat. In summer, grooming should be more thorough and frequent, and stabled animals also need more detailed daily attention.

GROOMING EQUIPMENT

1 Slicker block: Good for removing winter coat and loose hairs and polishing the coat.
2 Rubber curry comb: A softer brush for deeper cleaning of the hairy coat.
3 Uni groom: Massager and winter coat remover.
4 Mane comb: For finishing.
5 Curry comb: Used as a body brush for cleaning the coat.
6 Grooming mit: Excellent for removing the winter coat.
7 Cactus cloth mit: For stains, sweat marks and a final polish.
8 Comb: For combing the mane and tail.
9 Pulling comb: To tidy and shorten manes and strip out long hairs.
10 Hoof oil brush: For painting on hoof oil.
11 Hoof pick with brush: For picking out and brushing hooves.
12 Hoof pick: For picking out stones from hooves.
13 Sponges (2): One for the face and one for the rear of the pony.
14 Uni-groom: Good for massage, cleaning faces and sweat marks.
15 Sweat scraper: Sweat and excess water remover.
16 Curry comb: For manes and tails.
17 Dandy brush: Used for the initial grooming brush.
18 Body brush: Good for removing dust and mites from the coat.
19 Water brush: For applying water and brushing a wet coat.
20 Hoof brush: Small brush to get into the hoof grooves.
21 Face brush: Small brush for those delicate areas around the eyes and mouth.

BASIC GROOMING ROUTINE FOR A STABLED PONY

When grooming your pony, always face the pony's quarters, never away from them. Nor should you stand directly behind him or you may receive a shove or a kick! It is best to groom outside the stable where it is less dusty.

TYING UP

1 Tie your pony up to a string loop through a metal ring, using a head harness and halter, and a quick-release safety knot.

2 Pass the rope through the string tie-ring and make a loop with the loose end. Thread through the first loop.

3 Tighten it by pulling on the half-bow but leave the loose end hanging down. You can release the horse quickly if necessary.

PRE-GROOMING CLEAN

1 Wash off any major dirt, mud and stains with the water brush. Do not be rough.

2 Brush in firm strokes with the dandy brush to remove any remaining mud and crusted dirt.

3 Beginning at the neck and working downwards, rub in circular motions with the rubber curry comb.

GROOMING THE MANE

1 With the mane comb and your fingers, gently untangle and comb through the mane, taking care not to pull the hair out.

2 With the body brush, brush the mane over to other side so that the brush goes right through the hair down to the roots where grease can accumulate.

3 Brush the mane back over again to the original side, a little at a time. Afterwards, brush and comb the tail.

BODY BRUSH

1 Beginning at the top of the neck and working down, use the body brush, working in the direction of the hair.

2 After about a dozen strokes, scrape the brush on the teeth of a metal curry comb to clean out the bristles.

3 Alternatively, you can tap it against a wall or on the floor or, best of all, on a wooden board standing nearby.

SPONGING THE HEAD

1 Take the halter or head harness off the pony before brushing the head. If wished, throw the lead rope round the horse's neck to retain control.

2 With the body brush, gently brush the head. Don't forget to brush under the jaw and the ears.

3 With a damp sponge which is clean and soft and kept specifically for this purpose, sponge the eye area with clean, preferably warm, water. It should not be so wet that it gets water into the pony's eyes.

4 Rinse out the sponge and then sponge around the mouth and nostrils.

WASHING THE DOCK

1 With another damp sponge kept for this purpose, gently sponge the dock (the skin at the top of the pony's tail and above the anus).

2 Lift the tail while you sponge the area underneath. Take care not to muddle up the sponges!

CHECKING THE HOOVES

1 Brush off the hoof walls, checking for any splitting.

2 Pick out the sole of the hoof. Remove foreign bodies and check the frog. Look for any soggy, smelly areas of rot.

3 Paint on hoof oil to keep the wall strong and in good condition.

1
2 **3**

LAYING THE MANE

Using a damp water brush from which you have shaken out any excess water, brush the mane downwards from the roots to the ends of the hairs. This makes the mane look neat and tidy with the hairs lying flat against the horse's head and neck.

POLISHING

Finally, use the stable rubber all over the body to 'polish' the coat and give it a healthy, glossy finish. Always wipe the pony's body in the direction in which the coat lies.

WASHING

Although very dirty areas, say the tail, can be washed off and dried during the winter, full bathing should be reserved for warmer weather. Even on the hottest summer day, always use at least lukewarm water.

 Use a special horse shampoo.

 Do not get shampoo into the pony's eyes.

 Rinse and dry the pony thoroughly using towels.

 Walk the pony around until it is completely dry.

 Finish off by light grooming with a body brush.

 If, by then, the air has grown cooler, put on a sweat rug with a light sheet on top.

WASHING LEGS

There is much debate about washing ponies' legs as some animals on certain soils easily get inflamed, chafed skin around the pasterns ('mud fever') after a good day's squidging through the mire. In winter, ponies kept out of doors should have their legs washed only if they are badly clogged with mud. Don't clip any long hair off the back of the fetlocks. It is best to preserve the natural grease and hair protection of the coat during the bad weather. In summer, I prefer to wash off the legs if they are muddy and put stable bandages on the clean, wet legs overnight.

LEFT: *If your pony's legs are muddy in summer, you can wash them off with a brush and some lukewarm water.*

HOOF CARE

To examine a pony's hoof, you will need to pick up the foot. If you do this frequently, the pony will learn to lift the hoof for you, particularly if you always use a word like 'lift' or 'foot' when you are doing it. For safety's sake, always approach the pony from the front, run your hands over him and talk to him before checking the hooves.

TO LIFT A FOREFOOT

1 Stand close to the animal facing its rear.

2 Run your hand down smoothly from the pony's shoulder to the fetlock.

3 Hold the fetlock firmly and bend it back.

4 Catch the front rim of the hoof with your other hand.

TO LIFT A HIND FOOT

1. Approach the pony from the head, standing close to it.

2. Run your hand along the pony's back as you approach its rear.

3. Stand close to the hindquarters, facing the rear of the pony and pressed against the hind leg so you cannot get kicked. Run your hand down the skin from buttock to fetlock and grab the joint firmly. Lift the fetlock forwards and upwards so all the leg joints bend. Take hold of the hoof rim and tuck yourself well in to the pony's body.

CHECKING THE CONDITION

Check the condition of the hooves regularly, looking for splits in the hoof wall, cleaning out dirt and stones from the grooves alongside the frog and oiling the hoof as necessary. Do not use a hoof knife or penknife to pare away even flaking bits of the frog – you may inadvertently reduce frog pressure when the animal is walking or running. Frog pressure within the hoof is essential to good circulation and the health of the foot. Always leave frog trimming to the expert care of the blacksmith or vet.

SPECIAL CARE

In winter, if the pony is going out onto snow, apply a thick layer of grease to the soles of the hooves to prevent snow compacting there.

ABOVE: *A liberal application of grease to the sole of the hoof is wise on snowy winter days.*

If a pony has hooves whose walls seem to be prone to dryness and splitting, then supplementing its food with biotin, a member of the vitamin B group, can help. Biotin powder can be obtained from feed merchants, veterinary pharmacists and horse tack shops.

CHECKING THE SHOES

At your routine inspection of the pony's feet, keep an eye on the shoes. It is time to arrange an appointment with the blacksmith when:

A shoe has been lost, twisted, broken or is loose

The shoes are worn thin

The toes or heels of the hoof are beginning to overgrow the shoe

The pony seems to stumble more often than before.

Note: You will need a farrier to trim the pony's hooves every two to three months, depending on how much it is ridden and how quickly the hoof wall grows.

UNSHOD PONIES

An unshod pony will still need regular attention from the blacksmith. The hoof is a living tissue which is constantly growing. As the hoof wall grows longer, it has a tendency to crack with potentially serious results. Skilled trimming is called for. Wild equines, of course, never see a blacksmith, but they keep their hooves naturally trimmed as they constantly move over rough or rocky ground.

LEFT: *Holding a foot up in the correct way to inspect the undersurface. This hoof belongs to a one-year-old unshod pony.*

CLOTHING

Some basic clothing should always be available for your pony. Seasonal and sudden weather changes, occasions when an animal is off colour for some reason or has been exerting itself – at times like these you may need to quickly dress the pony up.

SWEATING AND CHILLS

When a pony is sweating heavily in the stable after exercise, watch out for chills. Avoid these by rubbing the animal thoroughly with towels or wisps of hay, then sprinkle some straw on the animal's back and cover with a light rug. After half an hour, remove the cover and towel or wisp again. A very hot and bothered pony should be walked around gently in the shade while covered with the straw and the rug.

BELOW: *This pony's New Zealand rug is the correct size and is properly fitted.*

PROVIDING A RUG

A waterproof (New Zealand) rug should be provided for ponies wintered outside. However, several types of rug are available and these are as follows:

New Zealand rug: This rug is the 'overcoat' of the pony used to protect it against wind and rain. Although a tough little Dartmoor pony will thrive happily unrugged in all weathers, it is best to rug up the more delicate souls, the older ones and any ponies that tend to be 'rheumaticky' – just like humans!

Stable rug: This rug is put on indoors in chillier weather. It may be quilted or padded and is best fastened on the body with surcingles rather than the more uncomfortable and old-fashioned broad strap (roller). If necessary, when the temperature drops lower, a blanket can be worn beneath the rug.

Sweat rug: The equine equivalent of the

human string vest. The holes in the mesh trap air which insulates the body. It is always used with a sheet (in warm weather) or a stable rug (in cold weather) on top.

▲ **Exercise sheet:** Often waterproof, the exercise sheet covers the back beneath the saddle and can be used to keep the pony dry on winter rides.

▲ **Summer sheet:** The equine equivalent of the human beach shirt, this lightweight sheet is used in warm weather to keep flies off the pony and for travelling.

TOP RIGHT: *A summer sheet is lightweight and is usually made of cotton. It is used in summer when travelling or for keeping off flies.*
RIGHT: *A sweat rug; the equine equivalent of the human's string vest.*
BELOW: *As well as the heavy duty rugs used for outdoor protection in winter, additional comfort can be provided by padded hoods.*

FITTING A STABLE RUG

A rug should be the right size for your pony. It should fall on each side to cover the belly, elbows and stifles and be long enough to cover the dock and buttocks. It should fit neatly over the shoulders, withers, ribs and croup. To get an idea of the correct size before buying a rug, measure the distance between the point of the breast and the point of the buttock.

1. Fold the rug in half (with the inside out) and approach the pony from the front.
2. Put the folded rug on the pony with its forward edge just in front of the withers.
3. Fold the rug back, pulling it slightly towards the rear to neaten the fit, and then fasten the belly straps.
4. Carefully go behind the pony and fasten the hind leg straps.
5. Fasten the front straps, taking care not to pull the rug forwards over the pony's coat.

SADDLES

When obtaining a saddle, take advice from experienced folk, preferably a master saddler. The saddle you choose will depend on your weight, your height, your pony's size and shape and also what you want to do with your pony. Do you want to compete in Pony Club events, do jumping and dressage, or just have fun hacking around the countryside?

Saddles must fit perfectly – at least as well as your own favourite comfortable shoes. Ill-fitting saddles can cause sores on the pony's back which can become chronic and difficult to eradicate. The best saddles are English and they can be 'made-to-measure' or off the peg. Measurements and 'fittings' to ensure that you get the right size are always essential (see opposite). You may fancy a second-hand saddle – if so, fine; but inspect it carefully for undue wear, a broken internal framework or flat, exhausted padding. An ill-fitting saddle will not only be painful for the pony but also will cause you to ride out of balance.

Saddle

Pommel
Stud
Waist
Cantle
Seat
Skirt
Saddle flap
Panel
Sweat flap
(underneath saddle flap)

Girth

Expanding
elastic section

Numnah
Padded
saddle cloth

Peacock irons

Rubber
quick release

Stirrups

Irons

Rubber grips

FITTING A SADDLE

It is essential that for your pony's health and your safety as a rider that the saddle is fitted correctly by a qualified professional saddler. The saddle must distribute your weight properly and contour the pony so as not to inflict pain or discomfort.

LEFT: The front arch of the saddle must conform to the pony's back for correct weight loading.
1 The front arch is too narrow.
2 The front arch is too wide.
3 The front arch is the correct size for the pony.

LEFT: The tree of the saddle (with the front arch) must conform exactly to the pony's shape as shown here.

LEFT: This saddle is too wide. If your weight is over the front arch, the saddle drops to find the wider part of the pony and the frame lifts off at the back, transferring weight to the front.

ABOVE: After riding and removing the saddle, the hairs of the pony's coat should lie in a natural line.

ABOVE: This saddle is correctly fitted and will thus spread the rider's weight properly over the pony's body.

PUTTING ON A SADDLE

If you are not saddling up inside the stable, then either tie the pony up or have it held by someone else. Correct application and settling of the saddle is most important, not only for your comfort and security but to ensure the pony doesn't develop saddle sores.

1 Approach the pony's near side, steadily talking gently to it. Hold the saddle with your right hand and forearm under the seat.

2 Place the saddle gently on the pony's withers, with the numnah beneath, if you are using one, and then slide it back into its correct position.

3 Go to the oft side, let down the girth straps and then return to the near side and take the straps from under the pony's belly.

4 Do up the girth straps slowly, beginning with the front one and putting the strap through the top slot of the buckle. Don't tighten the straps excessively. Put a finger under each strap to check for wrinkled skin.

5 Fasten the back girth strap and adjust the buckle guard. Pull it down over the buckles.

6 Give the girth a final check to ensure that it is tightened correctly and make sure that no skin is wrinkled below before running down the stirrups.

7 This picture shows a correctly fitted saddle with the girth and stirrups in the correct position.

BRIDLES AND BITS

Controlling and steering the pony is done by specialized pieces of harness and equipment that link the rider's hands to the animal's head and particularly its mouth. The mouthpiece or gag comes in a multitude of designs, some of which are specially appropriate for certain types of riding or for specific types of pony.

Bits

Eggbutt snaffle

French-link eggbutt

Loose-ring hollow mouth snaffle

Full-check Fuller snaffle

Continental 3-ring gag

Kimblewick (slotted)

Mullen-mouth pelham

Pelham roundings

Briddle

Snaffle bit

Noseband

Cheekpiece

Fly fringe
Fits on to the browband

Browband

Headpiece

Reins (attached to rings of the bit)

Attaches to bridle

Loop slips round pony's neck

Running martingale
Used to correct a pony that consistently carries its head too high.

Attaches to saddle

FITTING A BRIDLE

It is important for the pony's comfort and the rider's safety that the bridle fits correctly and is neither too big or too small, too loose or too tight. You can perform a few simple checks to ensure that this is the case. The best bit is the one that is kindest in allowing the pony to go forward under the correct control; the type used will depend on the pony's strength and temperament.

ABOVE: *Check that the cavesson isn't too tight. If you can't put a finger into the nose band, it may cut into the pony's nose.*

ABOVE: *Check the throat latch. You should be able to insert your hand sideways if it is fitted correctly.*

ABOVE: *Check the brow band. You should be able to insert a finger between it and the pony's head.*

ABOVE: *There should be about 6mm/¹/₄ in between the side of the pony's mouth and the side of the bit.*

RIGHT: *The bit should always fit snugly in the pony's mouth.*

PUTTING ON A BRIDLE

The bridle, the contraption of leather straps that fits a pony's head, must fit properly and effectively and be kept in good condition for the animal's comfort and wellbeing and also for your safety. Always take advice from an experienced rider or professional saddler when first buying your pony's bridle.

1 Standing on the near side of the pony, slip the reins over its head.

2 Hold the bridle in front of the pony's face and then guide the bit very gently into the mouth.

3 Bring the headpiece up over one and then the other ear.

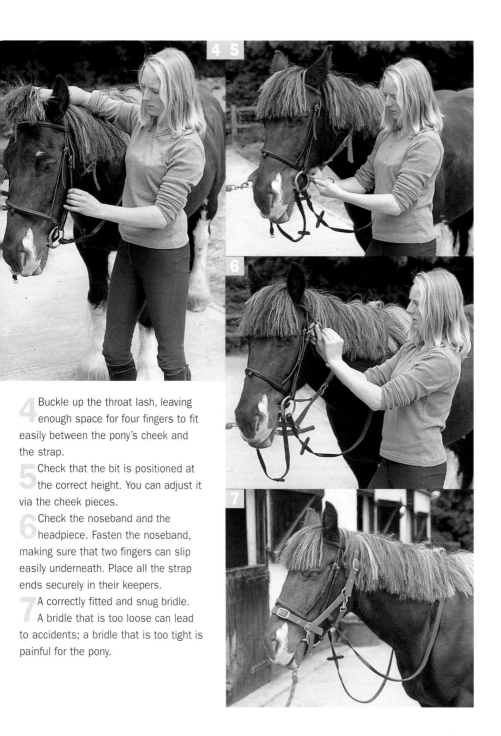

4 Buckle up the throat lash, leaving enough space for four fingers to fit easily between the pony's cheek and the strap.

5 Check that the bit is positioned at the correct height. You can adjust it via the cheek pieces.

6 Check the noseband and the headpiece. Fasten the noseband, making sure that two fingers can slip easily underneath. Place all the strap ends securely in their keepers.

7 A correctly fitted and snug bridle. A bridle that is too loose can lead to accidents; a bridle that is too tight is painful for the pony.

CHAPTER FIVE

HANDLING YOUR PONY

In many ways, the most important aspect of pony-keeping is learning how to handle the animal with skill and consideration. A happy duo of pony and owner, who are at ease with one another, is created by the firm but gentle application of touch, sound and sight – it's all about communication between you and the relationship that you build with one another.

APPROACHING YOUR PONY

Like many other animals, ponies are not very keen on unpredictable, erratic, excitable or noisy human beings. Their sensitive, watchful natures, stemming from wild ancestors who had to be ever ready to react instantaneously to prowling predators, make them nervous and resentful of loud folk who rush about, lose their temper, are spiteful or impatient. It may well be that their highly developed sense of smell enables them to detect changes in the chemical make-up of our human body odour when we become irate, panicky or stressed – scents that our weak human noses cannot pick up but which disturb their equine composure.

So in every aspect of pony handling, it is important to be calm, collected, predictable and steady, just like you want your pony to be. The more you practise it and do it, the easier and simpler it becomes. Who knows, if you get really good, you might even become a horse or pony 'whisperer'!

ON PUBLIC HIGHWAYS

Take maximum care at all times. Motor vehicles and their drivers can be big trouble for ponies. Sadly, not enough drivers drop their speed to no more than 24 kph/15 mph when approaching horses or ponies as recommended by the British Horse Society.

The basic rules for road safety are:

🔺 Go on the same side as the traffic, on the grass verge if there is one.

🔺 It is best to walk or trot. Do not canter on tarmac. Do not trot downhill. Never gallop.

🔺 Go slowly at a walking pace around corners.

🔺 If in doubt, lead the pony with you between him and the traffic. Keep talking to him.

🔺 Stand well back from level crossings when trains are due to pass. Ponies are usually frightened by the noisy locomotives and their carriages.

🔺 Always make courteous gestures of warning or thanks towards drivers.

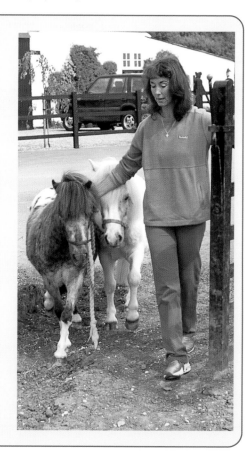

When approaching a pony, try to do so at an angle to the length of its body and not from behind or immediately in front – the animal's blind spots. Always speak to it as you approach steadily and then stroke or scratch it. Ponies soon recognise particular words, so you can issue commands like 'walk on', 'back' and, when it is necessary to reprove it, 'no'. Always give praise when it is due, in a gentle tone of voice. A correcting 'no' should be delivered firmly and sternly but without shouting. Be consistent at all times and your pony will soon learn the basics of good behaviour.

Rewards in the form of sugar lumps and the like should not be dispensed incessantly but rather from time to time, particularly when the pony cooperates in some way, such as allowing itself to be caught in the field.

BELOW: Three firm friends return home. When handling ponies, always be sure to stay calm and relaxed.

NOW FOR SOME IMPORTANT DON'TS:

▲ Never hit or grab at your pony.

▲ Never wrap a lead rope round your hand or wrist. If the pony made a dash, you could be pulled along and possibly severely injured.

▲ When tying up a pony, never attach it to a moveable object such as a gate, never tie it so short it cannot freely move its head, and never leave it alone when tied up. Use a secure quick-release knot such as the 'highwayman's hitch', attached to something like a loop of twine which will break if there is an emergency.

▲ When proffering a tidbit, do so with the palm of your hand held absolutely straight. Do not curl up your fingers – they may be mistaken for the goodies!

PUTTING ON A HARNESS

It is easy to tell if there is a good rapport between pony and owner, not least when it is time for harnessing. This should not be a haphazard, unpredictable confrontation but a quick, quiet, controlled and trouble-free coming-together of good pals.

1 Approach the pony from an angle, calmly and quietly and talking gently, with the bridle hidden from the pony's view.

2 Pass the lead rope round its neck to keep control if necessary.

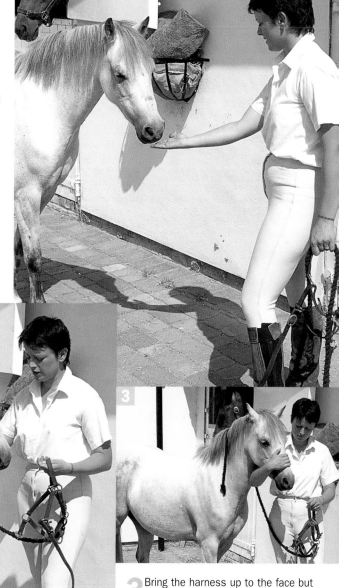

3 Bring the harness up to the face but not in a rush or jerkily.

4 and **5** Do up the head strap and check that all the parts of the harness are properly seated and neither too tight nor too loose.

LEADING YOUR PONY

This is usually done from its left (near) side, although there is nothing wrong with leading on the other (off) side. With your right hand, hold the lead rope some 20–30 cm/8–12 in from the pony's muzzle, and carry the rest of the length of rope in your left hand.

▲ Always walk beside the pony – never behind or in front of it.

▲ Do not wrap the lead rope round your left hand or arm.

▲ Get your pony accustomed to being led from its near or off side.

If leading your pony along a road, you should place yourself between it and the oncoming traffic (always walk on the side of the road that faces the traffic).

ABOVE: *Normally a pony is led from its near (left) side, holding the lead, rope or reins 20–30 cm/8–12 in from the animal's mouth in your right hand.*

ABOVE: *On roads, you should always place yourself between the pony and any approaching traffic, if necessary leading from the off (right) side.*
RIGHT: *Keep to the same side as the traffic travelling in your direction – if possible, use the grass verge.*

TURNING A PONY

You will often have to turn a pony in one direction or the other, particularly if you are checking it over for soundness. As with everything to do with ponies, there is a right way and a wrong way of doing this.

1 When turning a pony, always hold it quite close to the mouth.

2 Always turn the pony away from you. You are likely to get trodden on if you try turning it towards you.

3 Don't forget to talk gently to the pony all the time while turning it.

ENTERING A FIELD

This apparently simple procedure must always be done correctly if all sorts of mishaps and accidents are to be avoided.

1 You walk slightly ahead of your pony, without letting go of him, in order to deal with the catch on the gate.

2 Open the gate wide enough for both of you and lead the pony through, holding him fairly close to the mouth.

3 Close the gate while still holding the pony with one hand. Walk into the field a few paces and turn the pony round to face the gate. Let him stand for a few moments, slip off the head collar and let him go.

CATCHING A PONY

Like children who enjoy playing outdoors, most ponies sometimes would prefer not to be caught. It's a beautiful day, the grazing is toothsome at this time of year and I'm enjoying being nibbled by my old pal, the donkey – so why should I go off who knows where with my owner?

Some ponies are always easy to catch – but then there is the awkward squad. What should you do? Never try to chase or corner your pony. He'll enjoy the sport and he's nimbler than you. Be patient and bear rewards in the form of sugar lumps, etc. Always praise and fuss over him when, eventually, you succeed.

1 Enter the field and approach the pony steadily, certainly not dashing, and at an angle to his shoulder, holding the head collar behind your back or close to your side.

2 Talking gently all the time, cast the lead rope around his neck and then slide on the head collar.

3 Adjust the head straps. (Ponies that are consistently hard to catch can be left out in the field wearing a leather head collar with about 30 cm/12 in of rope attached.)

WARNING:

If going to the field with the intention of catching your pony and tacking him up and you find him standing conveniently by the entrance, do not, in a fit of laziness, attempt to put on the bridle or head collar by simply leaning over the gate. That way accidents happen!

CHAPTER SIX

HEALTHCARE

In general ponies are hale and healthy animals, not prone to ailments. With good management and nutrition, they live longer years and see less of the vet than most other domesticated animals. When things do go wrong, they are frequently afflictions related to the specialist anatomy and physiology of the equine. The responsible owner must know what to watch out for, and have a basic understanding of first aid, while never delaying unnecessarily getting professional help. The veterinary surgeon is a vital friend in looking after your pony's well-being. Seek out one whose practice contains plenty of equine work rather than another whose patients are 99 per cent small animals. Rely on veterinary advice when buying a new pony and see your vet at least once a year for routine vaccination shots.

HEALTHCARE

Just as you quickly realise that something is wrong when a friend or relative is feeling unwell, so with your pal the pony. When you have known one another for a little while, you will have no difficulty in spotting that he is a bit out of sorts. Every time you go to your pony, take a few moments to check him over. Look at, listen to, and, of course, as you should do whenever approaching him, touch the animal. It is best to run through a routine of check-points every day. You will quickly learn to detect anything abnormal.

DAILY CHECKLIST

⚘ Stand back a bit and look at the pony overall. Is he alert and bright and glad to see you? Are his posture and general behaviour normal?

⚘ Is the coat lying normally, dry and shiny and not 'staring' or sweaty?

⚘ Is the pony eating and drinking his normal rations with gusto?

⚘ Listen carefully. Any dry cough or wheezing? Is his breathing normal?

⚘ Are the eyes and nostrils free of discharge? Are the membranes that line the eyelids, nostrils and mouth moist and pale pink, not pallid, very red or dry?

⚘ Watch the pony passing urine; is it clear, pale yellow and voided without straining? Are the droppings of normal consistency – not too hard and not pasty or semi-liquid?

⚘ Is your pony standing and walking normally? Check the legs for puffiness or the appearance of lumps and bumps. Is each fore and hind leg symmetrical with its fellow on the opposite side?

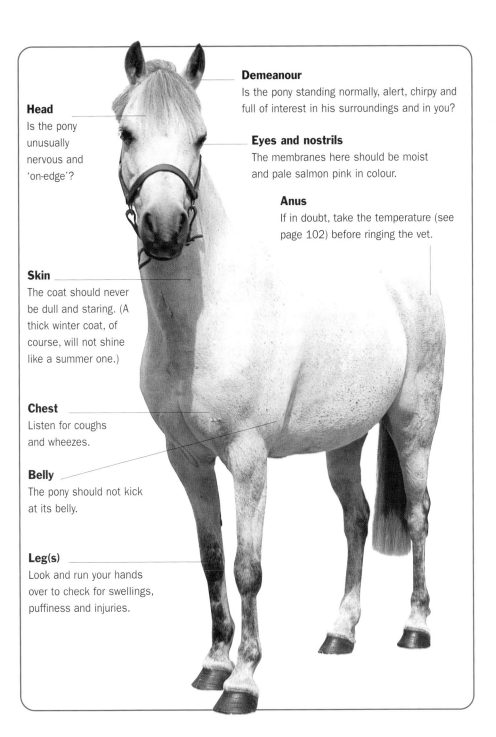

Head
Is the pony
unusually
nervous and
'on-edge'?

Demeanour
Is the pony standing normally, alert, chirpy and
full of interest in his surroundings and in you?

Eyes and nostrils
The membranes here should be moist
and pale salmon pink in colour.

Anus
If in doubt, take the temperature (see
page 102) before ringing the vet.

Skin
The coat should never
be dull and staring. (A
thick winter coat, of
course, will not shine
like a summer one.)

Chest
Listen for coughs
and wheezes.

Belly
The pony should not kick
at its belly.

Leg(s)
Look and run your hands
over to check for swellings,
puffiness and injuries.

GENERAL HEALTHCARE

TAKING THE TEMPERATURE

It isn't done by sticking a thermometer into your pony's mouth or under his foreleg. Put a halter or bridle on the animal and get someone to hold him. With one hand, hold the tail up as you stand close to the nearside hind leg. Insert gently into the anus an ordinary clinical thermometer which has been greased with petroleum jelly or olive oil. When it is well in, angle it so that the bulb is pressed against one wall of the rectum.

TAKING THE PULSE

To take a pony's pulse rate, normally 35 to 40 per minute, place your first and second fingers under the back of the lower jawbone. You will feel the artery pulsating beneath the skin just on the inside of the jaw, but it requires practice.

ABOVE: *To take the temperature, move aside the tail and gently insert a lubricated thermometer into the anus at an angle so it presses against the rectal wall.*

The normal temperature of the pony is around 38°C/100.2°F, higher than humans but lower than that of other domestic animals.

EXAMINING THE MOUTH

To look in an equine mouth (to inspect the teeth, for example), have the beast haltered or bridled and preferably held by someone else. Standing on the nearside, push your hand between the lips behind the incisors. There is a large toothless space here. Grab hold of the slippery, sliding tongue – it is rather like grasping a wriggling eel. Gently but firmly pull the tongue out between the lips on the near side and hold it. You can use

ABOVE: *A good position, gently restraining the head while examining the pony's mouth.*

the tongue gently to 'level' the mouth open, enabling you to look into its depths. A torch is often useful. Unless you are an expert, do not put your other hand into the space between the upper and lower molars – it is easy to have your fingers crushed painfully if your grip on the tongue slips, and sometimes even if it doesn't.

RESTRAINING YOUR PONY

Sometimes it is necessary to apply light restraint to an animal – when, for example, the vet is giving an injection or examining the body. The way to do this is to lift a fore leg and stand holding it in a position close to the animal and facing its tail. The correct way to pick up and hold a hind leg for inspection or cleaning a hoof is shown on page 74.

Restraining an animal by twitches and other contrivances is outside the scope of this book. This should rarely be necessary and is the province of experts. Many of the ingenious methods of days gone by – hobbles, casting, roping and gagging – are made elegantly redundant by the new range of modern tranquillizers and sedatives available to the veterinary surgeon should the occasion arise.

ADMINISTERING MEDICINES

The vet treats many horse ailments nowadays by injection. Drugs to be given by mouth are often formulated in special tasteless or pleasant-tasting granules or powders which can be mixed with mashes – even so, ponies have a good sense of taste and can be very finicky and suspicious over 'doctored' grub. Adding jam or treacle can mask an odd flavour in the food. Another ploy is to mix the drug with a few blocks of melted chocolate. Then let the chocolate set again in the refrigerator and present the sweetmeat to your pet with an innocent look on your face!

Giving large pills or boluses by means of a balling-gun is rare nowadays and should be left to the experts.

Drenching (pouring liquids into the animal) is not as easy as it sounds – usually it is the human who ends up drenched, with little or none of the medicament inside the nag. Do please, if you must drench your pet, try to avoid drowning it. Have it haltered and held by someone strong and reliable with its head as high as possible and in a straight line with its body. Use a metal or leather-covered drenching bottle; there is a danger of the strong cheek teeth breaking the neck of the stoutest beer or milk bottle. Push the neck of the bottle into the space between the incisor and cheek teeth and turn it towards the gullet. Pour in a little at a time to allow the animal time to swallow. Do not hold or have the tongue held. There is no rush – take it easy. You do not want to introduce liquid into the windpipe.

BANDAGING

Applying a stable bandage is a very simple procedure which is necessary when the pony's legs need some protection for any reason. Start with the bandage rolled with the tapes or fastening inside of the roll. Hold the end of the bandage against the leg with one hand and then go round and round with the other hand, overlapping each turn by two-thirds of the breadth of the bandage. Finally, tie the bandage around the legs with a neat, tight bow on the outside.

1 Always put a layer of padding under a bandage. Check that it fits well and lies smoothly before covering.

2 Have the bandage ready rolled before you begin bandaging the legs.

3 Hold the end of the bandage with one hand and then slowly begin to unroll it around the leg, pressing firmly.

4 Each turn of the bandage should overlap the previous one by two-thirds.

5 It's best to start at the top of the padding. When you reach the bottom of it, you should go back up again.

6 Fasten the bandage firmly, but not too tightly, with tapes or Velcro. You should be able to slip a finger down inside the bandage.

Protective boots

Boots of various types are used to protect the pony's legs from damage. This can occur when jumping or when there is a tendency for one leg to brush against another ('brushing') or when 'over-reaching', the hind legs clipping the heels of the fore feet when in motion.

1   As with bandages, boots should fit snugly but not too tightly. You should be able to slip a finger down inside them.

2   Always fasten the straps of the boot on the outside of the leg.

MEDICAL PROBLEMS

It is not my intention in this little book even to attempt a manual on the diagnosis and treatment of equine ailments by the lay owner. The modern medical approach to sick ponies is a complex professional task that should be left to the veterinary surgeon. The days of 'cure-all' bottles of physic, blood-letting and mustard plasters have been left far behind and it is unfair on the animal, inefficient, and often dangerous and downright illegal for unqualified people who 'reckon to know a bit about 'osses' to be allowed to play at doctors with such precious creatures. The owner's responsibility is to be alert for signs of trouble, to supply good nursing and supportive treatment when the vet has examined the pet, and to prevent problems, rather than cure them, through good stockmanship.

Ponies have some advantages and a few disadvantages compared to horses when it comes to healthiness. Ponies are generally hardy and trouble-free but are particularly prone to recurrent bouts of laminitis. They never develop roaring or whistling, the windpipe troubles of their bigger relatives. And they tend, on average, to live longer than horses.

SIGNS OF ILLNESS

You will have come to know the personality and temperament of your pet, his attitudes and his general approach to life. The first signs of trouble are ones that you will detect – alterations in the routine, the normal. There may be a change of mood to dullness or tetchiness, a vague sluggishness or a curious 'something' in the way he moves. More obvious symptoms will relate to one of the major organ systems of his body, such as changes in the appearance of his droppings, slowness of eating or lack of appetite, change in the rhythm of his breathing and its intensity, discharges at one of the orifices of his body or the development of troublesome areas on his skin or in the eyes. Many diseases of the horse affect more than one system in the body and diagnosis generally needs professional techniques.

TOOTH PROBLEMS

Your pony will rarely need dental treatment, although decayed teeth, root infections and the like do occur. The commonest fault is that the cheek teeth either develop sharp points or become worn down until their grinding surfaces are smooth. These alterations to the tooth profile can cause discomfort or simply difficulty in chewing food. They are seen most often in old animals but also occur from time to time in youngsters. The signs are slowness in eating and a tendency to sloppiness with the dropping of food, particularly hay. The vet can quite easily file off points or roughen smooth-surfaced teeth with a tooth-rasp. It is a simple, painless procedure which may have to be repeated every three or four months.

EYE PROBLEMS

There are many different eye ailments. The commonest are inflammation of the cornea and conjuctiva caused by injuries, by foreign bodies, such as grit or hay awns, or by

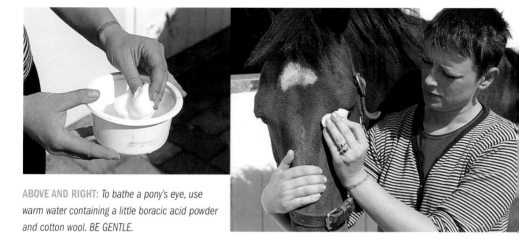

ABOVE AND RIGHT: *To bathe a pony's eye, use warm water containing a little boracic acid powder and cotton wool. BE GENTLE.*

straightforward bacterial infection. Watch out for any discharge or excessive water from an eye or eyes, redness of the 'white' of the eye and any bluish haziness of the normally transparent cornea. At the first sign of any such abnormality, call the vet and meanwhile bathe the eye gently with a warm (body heat) solution of one teaspoonful of boracic acid crystals dissolved in a teacup of water. Don't

BELOW: *In summer, you can carefully apply some fly-repellent cream close to BUT NOT IN the eye.*

let matter build up round the eyelashes and on the lids as it will only make things worse. If flies are paying a lot of attention to sore eyes, apply a little dimethyl; phthalate cream with your finger to the skin of the eyelids. If the eye is very sore and watering profusely, the animal would be best in a shady loose-box until treatment begins to take effect.

CHEST PROBLEMS

Respiratory disease is common in equines. Signs may include one or more of the following:

- ▲ Nasal discharge
- ▲ Coughing
- ▲ Dullness
- ▲ Sweating
- ▲ Fever
- ▲ Fast or heavy breathing.

There are several different types of chest problem, each with its own causes and symptoms, so early diagnosis is essential for correct treatment and proper recovery. Your job is to move the sick animal to a dry, warm but well-ventilated, dust-free stable. No work should be done and it is often best to keep the animal lightly rugged-up. A bran mash each day helps keep the bowels open. Provide easily digested food, soft new hay and plenty of lukewarm water. Don't waste time administering cough medicines or other potions before calling the vet.

Equine influenza and bacterial infections

Several viruses can produce chest ailments in equines: the most familiar is equine influenza. The virus attacks ponies and donkeys as well as horses but it can be guarded against by preventive vaccination. Initially two doses are given three to six weeks apart with a third dose five months later and annual boosters thereafter. Some makes of vaccines are administered at somewhat different intervals. The bacterial infections of the chest are treated by the vet using injectable antibiotics and other drugs such as mucus liquifiers. Antibiotics are rarely given by mouth to equines, so as not to disturb the friendly digestive bacteria in the intestines, but sulphonamides and similar chemicals can be administered as powders mixed with food or as an oral paste in special syrups.

Broken wind

Cases of so-called 'broken wind' in equines are the chronic result of dust from mouldy hay or straw. There is no true cure, and prevention is the watchword – don't buy poor, damaged hay or straw, make sure stables are well-ventilated, and don't store fodder above or very close to the animal's living quarters.

Lung-worms

These are a particular risk in donkeys and can easily spread from them to their pony or horse stable companions. Newly-arrived donkeys should be wormed with a drug such as fenbendazole

before coming into contact with other equines, and all donkeys, ponies and horses on the premises should be wormed regularly together at intervals of, say, three months.

TUMMY PROBLEMS

Colic

The most famous illness of horses, this is actually acute indigestion and comes in several forms, some mild, some serious and violent. The causes of colic are related to the management of the diet: over-feeding, abrupt changes of diet and unsuitable foodstuffs, such as wheat, mouldy food, too much water given to a hot and tired animal, watering after a feed and worms, are the commonest causes.

▲ **Symptoms** A pony with colic shows the symptoms of abdominal pain:
▲ It stops feeding
▲ It looks round at its flanks
▲ It kicks at its belly
▲ It lies restlessly down, soon to stand up and then just as soon lie down again, unable to find ease or comfort
▲ It may stand with hind legs apart as if trying to pass urine and, in severe cases where the pain is intense, may throw itself around alarmingly.

The pain is caused by spasms in the intestine walls and the presence of gas which disturbs the bowels. Few or no droppings are passed. If the bowel spasms are so intense that the intestinal wall twists or telescopes, cutting off its blood supply, the outcome is frequently fatal. Quick veterinary treatment, however, usually results in a complete recovery.

▲ **Treatment** Your job is to send for the veterinary surgeon and then try to relieve the animal's discomfort as much as possible. Keep it warm by light rugging and walk it around, preferably indoors if possible. Spread plenty of thick bedding about in case the animal goes down. Although the vet will use drugs given by injection or by stomach-tube,

ABOVE: *A lightly-rugged pony is walked around while waiting for the vet to arrive.*

there is no harm in your trying to drench into your pet four tablespoons of the common human anti-diarrhoea mixture, kaolin and morphine, which is diluted with 300 ml/½ pint of warm water. Don't give any laxatives until the vet has been consulted.

Note: You will notice that I do not mention vomiting as a symptom of colic (or any other tummy trouble in equines). The reason is that horses, ponies and donkeys cannot vomit.

Diarrhoea

This is very uncommon in ponies. It can be caused by infections, sudden alterations in the diet, poisons such as acorns (when taken in large amounts), insecticides, mouldy food or, most important of all, particularly in the young animal, worms. The condition always requires quick professional attention. Until the vet arrives, keep the animal indoors and warm and allow it to drink as much lukewarm water as it wishes. There is no harm in your trying to drench in a cupful of keopectate emulsion diluted with 300 ml/½ pint of warm water.

WORMS

The horse family suffers from the attentions of many sorts of worms. Of the three main groups, round-worms (including lung-worms), tape-worms and fluke-worms, it is usually the round-worm that causes all the trouble and sometimes death in horses, ponies and donkeys. The worms live not just in the bowels but also in other places, such as lungs, tendons, skin and even inside the eye. Intestinal worms spend part of their life-cycle migrating through the body via the bloodstream, and the effects of their wanderings on the blood vessels can be severe and sometimes suddenly fatal.

Equines have their own particular worms, as do dogs, cats, sheep and cattle. These worms are not interchangeable between species. Although the large white round-worms, which can be 30 cm/12 in long and 6 mm/¼ in thick and are a particular threat to foals, are easily seen in the droppings, other worm species are even more dangerous and not as easily visible.

▲ **Prevention** Ponies should receive regular worming medicine at least once every three months. There are various effective wormers available from the vet, tack shop or chemist. The modern ones, such as fenbendazole or mebendazole, will kill all the major species of dangerous worms. The drug can be given as a powder mixed with the feed or as a paste squirted onto the tongue from a handy disposable oral doser. In order to avoid the worms developing resistance to your worming drug, it is quite a good idea to change the type of medicine from time to time. With zebras under my care, I like to alternate fenbendazole with pyrantel at the regular worming sessions.

BELOW: *One common way of worming a pony is by using a special worming syringe whose contents are squirted into the animal's mouth.*

TETANUS

Tetanus is a very serious disease which sometimes occurs in man and other domestic and wild animals, but is a particular threat to equines. The germ enters the body through a wound, usually a badly aerated, soil-contaminated puncture, although it may also gain access to apparently uninjured animals, probably from the bowel via abrasions or ulcerations of the intestinal wall.

🔺 **Symptoms** These are of progressive stiffness due to spasm of the body muscles.
🔺 The limbs become rigid and somewhat splayed, like the legs of an old-fashioned milking stool.
🔺 The tail becomes raised and the third eyelid moves over the eyeball.
🔺 Increasing difficulty in opening the mouth due to the spasm of the jaw muscles gives the common name of the disease – lockjaw.
🔺 Bright lights and noise increase the involuntary movement of the muscles.

🔺 **Treatment** With vigorous treatment and careful nursing about a half of tetanus cases can be expected to recover. The vet will tackle the disease by trying to locate and disinfect the site of entry of the bacteria, and by administering antibiotics, tetanus anti-serum and special muscle-relaxant drugs. The owner has much to do, nursing the animal in quiet, dimly-lit quarters, giving nourishment by any route possible and even supporting the patient in slings.

🔺 **Prevention** Your chief responsibility is to prevent the risk of tetanus in your pet. Make sure it is vaccinated against the disease and that it receives yearly booster injections. Unvaccinated animals which are wounded

VACCINATIONS

Every pony should be vaccinated against tetanus (see left) and equine influenza (see page 108), most particularly if you hear of an outbreak in your area. The vaccines can be administered to healthy animals by the veterinary surgeon, in most cases from the age of three to four months.

The timing of when best to first vaccinate a young pony will depend on a number of factors, such as the degree to which a young foal derives some immunity in the form of antibodies against a disease from its mother; your vet will advise you about this. Combined tetanus/influenza vaccines are now available.

You must remember to follow up the initial vaccination course with annual booster shots that maintain the protection. Other vaccines which are used under special circumstances are those against equine herpes viruses which can cause another variety of respiratory disease and rabies. These are not given routinely to ponies in the UK; your vet will advise you should they be deemed necessary. Rabies shots, for example, would be wise if you are taking your pony to countries where rabies exists in wildlife.

There are other, less common, complaints against which a pony can be protected by vaccination. Whatever you do, when you first acquire a pony, DISCUSS IMMUNIZATION WHICH IS APPROPRIATE TO THE AREA IN WHICH YOU LIVE WITH YOUR VETERINARY SURGEON.

need the immediate but short-term protection of an injection of tetanus anti-serum, together with the first dose of tetanus vaccine to begin long-term immunity.

SKIN DISEASES

There are many kinds of skin disease in equines, and abnormal changes in the texture and appearance of the skin can result from the invasion of microbes, parasites of many different species, foreign bodies, allergies, sensitivity to light induced by eating certain plants, warts and other growths, dietary factors and other things.

Parasites

If you see parasites, such as lice, ticks or (rarely) fleas, on your pet, dusting him with some permethrin powder or shampooing with a piperonyl and pyrethrum horse shampoo, both obtainable from the chemist or tack shop, will eradicate the problem. Other types of skin ailment needs professional diagnosis.

Saddle sores

A fair number of sores in the saddle region are caused, particularly in riding ponies, by ill-fitting tack. You must buy the best tack you can afford and have it fitted to your pony by an experienced saddler. It must be properly cleaned and maintained and stored in a dry, clean, orderly place. Buying tack 'off the peg' without trying it for size, fit and comfort on the animal is like buying false teeth by mail order.

RIGHT: *The main way to avoid saddle sores: putting on a well-fitting saddle with a numnah beneath it in the correct manner.*

LAMENESS

Horses and ponies evolved their extraordinary limbs to enable them to speed away from danger, In doing so, they modified their legs and feet so that they now walk and run on the equivalent of one toe (or finger) on each leg, the nail having been enlarged into a hoof. A side effect of this development has been a susceptibility to lameness – everything depends on the simple 'toe' and it can easily be damaged or develop faults.

Lameness is common in ponies and it can strike without warning. It is no respecter of equine persons, and is as likely to lay low a racing thoroughbred as an Irish tinker's long-suffering pony. It may be caused by a number of factors, including wounds, bruising, damage to muscles, nerves, tendons, ligaments or bones, dislocations, arthritis-type conditions (e.g. splints, ringbones and navicular disease), inflammation of the bags of lubricating liquid that protect a joint or tendon (e.g. windgall, capped hocks and bog spavins), a disease of the foot (e.g. laminitis and canker), damage to the hoof wall, shoeing faults, skin disease (e.g. grease and mud fever) and bone disease (e.g. rickets).

The affected area can be in the groin, back muscles, legs or feet. The causes of lameness vary widely and the diagnosis and treatment may be relatively simple or extremely difficult. Early treatment is essential to prevent acute conditions (those that come on suddenly and don't last long) from becoming chronic (long-term and well set in).

🔺 **Treatment** The veterinary treatment of lameness depends on the nature of the problem, ranging from drug therapy to surgical methods of repairing damaged tissues or removing diseased areas. However, sometimes the co-operation and skill of the local blacksmith is called for in order to relieve certain lameness in ponies by the fitting of special 'surgical' shoes.

🔺 **Prevention** Your job is to watch out for any signs of lameness in your pony and to act promptly, and also to ensure that your animal's legs and feet are always kept in good condition. Regular examination of the limbs and feet, coupled with attention from time to time by the blacksmith, who will tidy up hooves that are tending to overgrow and will fit good shoes to ponies at appropriate intervals, are essential preventative measures in avoiding this common health problem.

ACUTE LAMENESS

In cases of acute lameness where you can locate the site your action should be:

1 Rest the animal indoors.

2 Bathe the affected part in cold water, hose with cold water or apply ice-bags.

3 If the lameness is in a limb, apply one of the special Animalintex dressings, available from the tack shop or chemist, or wrap it in cloths soaked in a cooled infusion of comfrey leaves.

Note: Don't start rubbing on liniments or other potions or administering medicines that were perhaps left over from other cases of lameness. Call the vet.

LAMENESS – TELL-TALE SIGNS

I am not expecting you to be an expert diagnoser of the seats of lameness. However, there are some important tell-tale signs that you must be on the watch for.

▲ At the first sign of abnormal action or movement, try to locate which part of the body or limb is affected.

▲ If an animal is lame in the fore leg, watch it from in front: it will 'nod' its head downwards as the good fore leg strikes the ground.

▲ If a hind leg is in trouble, view from behind: the point of the hock of the good leg travels a greater distance up and down than the point of the hock on the bad leg.

Of course, these are the simplest cases. If the trouble is in the back, the pelvis or in more than one leg at the same time, things can be more difficult to identify. Don't try to guess.

▲ You can run your hand over the body and particularly the limbs, looking for tender spots or unusual swellings.

▲ You can inspect carefully for wounds, for signs of disease on the surface and for areas that are unusually hot, as compared perhaps with the corresponding parts on the opposite side of the pony's body.

▲ Check the hoof for picked-up stones and for signs of injury or disease on the sole or frog.

ABOVE: *Watching the pony's action when it is moving on a hard surface with someone else leading it is the best way to check for signs of lameness.*

PONIES AND LAMINITIS

Laminitis is a common complaint of ponies, particularly in the spring and in over-fed little fatties! It can also be induced by some form of indigestion, a sudden change of diet or food that is 'off' in some way, or in animals with a feverish disease such as pneumonia, womb inflammation or retention of the afterbirth after foaling. The disease is an inflammation of the horn-producing tissues below the hoof and it occurs normally in all four or at least two feet. It is very painful and the animal stands miserably, often with the fore feet as far forward as possible and the hind feet pulled well under the body. It literally hasn't got a foot to stand on – all are equally punishing – and it doesn't like the feet to be handled or picked up. The temperature is often raised by two to four degrees.

BELOW: Keep the sick pony warm with plenty of soft bedding and even some light rugging if required.

🔺 **Treatment** Laminitis cases need veterinary treatment and modern drugs in order to relieve the pain and suppress the inflammation. Your job is to rest the animal indoors on lots of thick, soft bedding or, if available, damp clay. Keep the animal warm, if necessary by lightly rugging it, and encourage it to drink plenty of water. A bran mash to keep the bowels open should be given each day.

🔺 **Prevention** Ponies on rich pasture in spring or ones that are spoilt with constant over-feeding may have recurrent attacks of laminitis which gradually deform the feet; they become 'slipper-shaped', with long, concave hoof-walls that are grooved with distinct horizontal rings. At this stage veterinary treatment can only compensate for the altered action of the damaged feet by surgical shoeing and by regular attention from the blacksmith, who will attempt to bring the foot little by little back towards it normal shape by cutting back the toe and shaving the hoof-walls at the sides and heels to encourage contact of the frog with the ground and therefore better circulation of the blood in the foot.

It is your responsibility to avoid over-feeding, particularly in the spring, and to exercise your pony. You may have to slim your pony by reducing drastically the amount of concentrates in its diet or even, if it is feeding purely on lush spring grass, allowing it only a couple of hours grazing per day, the rest of the time being spent in the stable or out exercising. However, all this is easier said than done. Owners find it very difficult to be tough with their pets but it really is in everybody's best interests – it can save your animal a great deal of suffering and a shortened life.

BELOW: *Too much lush new spring grass can cause problems with ponies' health and general wellbeing. Limit the amount of time they spend in the field.*

BREEDING

This book is not for those who want an entrée into the world of thoroughbred breeding with all the attendant mumbo-jumbo, advanced science and multitude of problems. Ponies left to their own devices and running wild have less trouble in reproducing their kind than do any of the pampered blood-horses of Newmarket or Kentucky. They find it no bother at all to have 95 per cent of their mares conceiving and nearly that percentage giving birth to live foals without the need for human assistance or interference. The pony-lover who wants a foal about the place won't find it quite as easy as wild pony herds but it is still a fairly simple business with a success rate that, on average, produces one young, survivable nag every two years.

PREGNANCY

A horse's gestation period is eleven months. Mating occurs when the mare is in season (oestrus) and will accept the male. Oestrus occurs at intervals of three weeks between March and September and lasts for four to eight days. The longest pregnancy period of all equines is that of the Grevy's zebra – about 390 days!

Signs of a mare in season

What starts all this off is the increasing hours of daylight in spring. The light affects the eyes which pass a message to the brain which notifies the pituitary gland below the brain. The pituitary gland then sends a chemical hormone through the blood to the ovary and tells it to get busy gathering up egg cells.

When a mare enters oestrus she becomes 'different'. She may seem more excitable than usual or more placid. She stands from time to time with hind legs apart as if wanting to pass urine. The tail is raised and the lips of the vagina wink open and closed. She squeaks, fidgets, kicks and squirts small amounts of urine if touched on the back or flanks. These symptoms are more exaggerated if a male is around, even though she may reject him and kick him in the first few days of heat. Later she is more compliant and allows mating. The best time to conceive is two days before the end of oestrus but, as you don't know in advance when it will end, you should if possible allow mating to occur every other day while the mare will accept the male.

Young males are fertile by the time they are two years old and females can conceive at one year of age, though this is not a good idea; it is best to wait until females are at least two before mating. One of the most fertile heat periods is the so-called 'foaling heat', which happens about one week after the mare gives birth. Statistically, more mares lose foals conceived at this time, and some vets have reservations about the practice, but you can use this heat if you are

intent on repeat breeding.
If your mare doesn't come
into heat and you really want a
foal, consult your vet. There are many
causes of infertility and, after a thorough
examination, the vet may prescribe hormone
or other forms of therapy.

Pregnancy detection

From three weeks after mating, the vet may
often be able to do a manual inspection via
the rectum if the mare is big enough. A blood
test can be done by the vet between the forty-
fifth and ninetieth day of the suspected
pregnancy. A urine test can be carried out by
the vet after the 150th day.

THE BIRTH

The udder enlarges in the last months of
pregnancy and a waxy discharge accumulates
on the teats a few days before the big event.
Milk may actually run from the teats during
this time. The tissues around the head of the
tail slacken, and the vaginal opening becomes
larger and more soft. Foaling is a private affair
– mares like, if possible, to perform the
miracle alone at night and, if watched, often
seem able to hold their foal back until the
human intruder has to go off for a bite to eat
or a cup of tea.

The time taken in giving birth from the
onset of the first visible contraction is
normally between 30 and 60 minutes. As
contractions intensify, the mare becomes
restless and often shows signs as if she had
colic. Do not interfere.

Once a foal is delivered, you can interfere
only if the placental membranes are
obstructing its nostrils (just tear a hole in
them) but otherwise let the foal rest for a
quarter of an hour. Never hurry separation of
the umbilical cord linking dam and foal – it
will break when eventually one or the other
stands up.

The placenta, or afterbirth, follows the
birth of the foal within one to three hours. It
must all come away within 12 hours, otherwise
veterinary advice is essential. If you find
a rubbery brown 'stone' in the afterbirth
material, don't be alarmed. It is a hippomane
– an agglomeration of cellular waste from the
placental fluid. It is not significant but was
once considered to be of enormous medical
and magical value.

But suppose the mare is obviously in labour
but no foal has been fully delivered within the
normal space of one hour – what then? Call
the vet if two hours have passed from the
time the first contractions were seen and the
birth has not been completed. The vet can
correct problems of foaling manually, with
drugs or exceptionally by Caesarean section
under general anaesthetic. But I must
emphasise that the vast majority of foalings
pass off without a hitch.

REARING

Foals are usually reared happily by their
mothers without any need for human
interference. Should difficulties arise, consult
your vet at once. There are, however, two
points of general importance should the need
to bottle-feed a foal arise:

1 The first milk (colostrum) produced by the
mare in the 48 hours after foaling is
essential for a healthy foal. Try to get some
(even if it is only a dessertspoonful) into the
baby, if necessary in emergencies by milking
the mare. 'Banks' of stored frozen colostrum
do exist for special cases of need and you

CASTRATION

This process is also known as 'gelding' or 'cutting'. Male ponies are castrated by surgical removal of their testicles harmlessly under an anaesthetic if they are not required for breeding. The best age for the operation is when the animal is two years old although it can be done as early as three months or much later in life if necessary. The operation does not take more than a few minutes to perform. The idea is to avoid unruly behaviour as they get older, particularly when there are females in heat in the neighbourhood, although some uncastrated males do live lives of utter decorum and have the most gentlemanly characters.

can be put in touch with one via your vet if absolutely necessary.

2 Cow's milk is too rich for orphan foals and contains less sugar. To use cow's milk in an emergency, add three parts water (or, better, lime water – not lime cordial) to two parts milk and mix two teaspoonfuls of brown sugar to each 600 ml/1 pint of the mixture.

ACCIDENTS

Accidents will happen: collisions with fences, wire, glass and the like, injuries in the field or on the road, mishaps in the stable or when one animal meets another. For most accidents you will usually need to consult the vet, but you must have some idea of how to perform some simple first aid.

WOUNDS

These can be of all sizes, shapes and severities from mere pin-pricks to extensive lacerations. Whatever the cause or nature of the wound, there is a danger of infection developing. So, where the damage is more than very minor, it is wisest to call the veterinary surgeon who can protect the beast with injections or oral forms of anti-bacterial drugs.

First aid

This consists of stopping bleeding, which is achieved best by pressure from a pad of cotton wool, clean cloth or even simply a clenched fist, and after cleaning the wound gently with warm water and a weak solution of antiseptic, such as Betadine or Dettol. However, if the wound is more than 1 cm/^{1}/$_2$ in or so in length (and in the case of smaller wounds, those that are located on special areas such as eyelids), the vet will probably need to put in a few nylon or other synthetic sutures. If there is a chance of this, don't gunge up the area with smelly

BELOW: *Cleaning a wound with antiseptic solution. Bleeding is controlled by applying firm pressure on a pad of cotton wool or gauze.*

antiseptic ointment after cleaning. If you must put something on, then use a sulphonamide power (a very useful combination of sulphonamide and a blow-fly repellent is Negasunt, available from your vet).

If the wound is in a convenient site, such as a limb, then you can cover it with a light dressing, secured by bandaging.

There is always a risk of tetanus (lockjaw) in equines, particularly where wounds are deep, penetrating punctures that don't expose the damaged tissues to much air and which may be contaminated with dirt (see page 111). The tetanus bacterium thrives in airless wound, particularly if there are chalky soil particles around. Tetanus can be introduced through the most insignificant-looking punctures which do not bleed or through 'nail-pricks' hidden under a shoe.

Consequently, all equines should always be protected against the disease by being vaccinated with the tetanus vaccine. The initial course is normally two injections at an interval of four to six weeks, with a booster shot a year later and then every three years or if an injury occurs.

BRUISES AND SPRAINS

You should tackle these injuries as soon as they happen in order to stop them becoming established and turning slowly into other, more serious, things. Both may present themselves as tender areas, possibly puffy and warm, and with resultant lameness if involving a limb. Your job is to stop the bleeding within the damaged zone and to soothe the effects of the inflammation. Apply ice-packs or cold water sponges, or hose the part with cold water for 20 or 30 minutes. Then either apply the special wet dressing called Animalintex, if

ABOVE: *Hosing down a sprain. Use cold water soon after it occurs; warm water if it has been there for longer than a few hours.*

possible, or bandage firmly. The bandage restricts bleeding and fluid swelling of the tissues and gives support.

Note: Do not rub liniments on new injuries.

There is no reason why you shouldn't spray the affected area with a human-type pain-killing aerosol of the sort used for burns, but note that lots of equines detest aerosols of any kind because they emit an irritating ultrasonic whine which is inaudible to humans but easily picked up by pony ears. Rest the animal. If the trouble persists for more than a day or two at the most, call the vet.

SERIOUS ACCIDENTS

Should you be unlucky enough to have your pet involved in a serious accident, there are one or two basic things for you to do. If it is unable to rise or cannot walk, do not force it – send for the veterinary surgeon and stay at the animal's head, talking quietly and stroking it to reassure it. Cover it with a rug, sprinkled hay or your jacket to keep it warm.

▲ Don't try bottling anything into the animal although if there is some water and sugar handy, see if it can drink a little voluntarily.

▲ If there is major bleeding, control it with pressure at the point of haemorrhage by any means, including your knotted fist.

▲ Don't fiddle about with major injuries such as fractures; you may inflict more pain and shock. When the vet arrives, he will have injections such as pethidine to relieve pain and quick-acting sedatives or injectable anaesthesia if necessary.

FRACTURED LIMBS

These don't necessarily mean that the animal must be destroyed. Pet ponies aren't expected to win races like thoroughbreds and are much lighter built than their bigger relatives; racehorses need to have perfect legs and are unlikely to run brilliantly after a break, while their size can make their healing a long, difficult process. Many fractures in equines can now be mended by internal fixation (special metal rods to hold broken bones together) and devices such as tough plastic casts – rather than plaster of Paris which isn't really strong enough to use on anything but foals and tiny ponies. Healing may take many months and the treatment is often expensive; your vet will examine the animal and advise you after determining the type and extent of the fracture what is the kindest thing to do.

Lastly, don't panic. Keep calm – your pet depends on you to keep your head and think clearly.

EUTHANASIA

If an animal has to be euthanased, the veterinary surgeon will do this task humanely, without fuss and only for very good reasons. A merciful shot from a gun is instantaneous in its effect, but if you prefer another method you can ask your vet to give a painless overdose of anaesthetic intravenously. This technique has a drawback for those owners who, once their animal has died, quite properly wish to realise any residual carcass value: the flesh will be unfit for consumption by man or beast because of its content of anaesthetic.

Enough of this gloom! It is more than likely that your pony will thrive and live on to a ripe old age without any unpleasant incidents. Wild ponies and asses don't live much beyond twenty or twenty-five years, with the occasional individual reaching the low thirties, but perhaps your pony will challenge the longevity record for a domesticated equine – no less than sixty-one years!

GLOSSARY

Bay
Red-brown colour of the body with black mane, tail and lower legs ('points').

Blaze
A broad white stripe running down the face.

Blister
An irritant medication applied to certain chronic lumps or injuries to bring healing blood to the part.

Broken wind
Chronic lung damage causing 'heaving' breathing and cough.

Brushing
The knocking of one leg by its opposite number when the pony is moving.

Cantle
The back of the saddle.

Cast
When a pony is unable to get up.

Cavesson
A nose band.

Chaff
Chopped straw or straw/hay mix.

Chestnut
Ginger-red colour of the body with similar or lighter mane and tail.

Clicking
The sound of one foot, usually the hind, coming into contact with the other. Clicking can cause damage and the pony may need boots or remedial shoeing.

Colic
A painful stomach/bowel condition.

Colt
An uncastrated male under three years of age.

Cow-hocked
The hock joints turn outwards.

Crib-biting
A 'vice' where a bored, stabled pony nibbles wood or other solid objects.

Dam
A pony's mother.

Dock
The top of the tail that contains the bony vertebrae.

Dorsal stripe
A dark stripe along a pony's back.

Dun
Brown, gold or cream body colour with darker mane, tail and lower legs.

Fetlock
A projection behind and above the hoof.

Filly
A female under three years of age.

Firing
An antiquated veterinary technique of inserting hot needles into chronically damaged sinews, but of doubtful value.

Forging
Hitting the underneath of the fore foot with the toe of the hind foot. This condition needs remedial shoeing.

Frog
The V-shaped pad on the sole of the hoof.

Gait
The leg movement of a pony.

Gelding
A castrated male.

Grazing muzzle
This is used to restrict a pony's intake of grass on pasture.

Grey
A coat colour produced by a mix of white and dark hairs.

Halter

A head-harness, which is often made of rope, for leading the pony or tying it up.

Hand

A unit of measurement for ponies, equivalent to 10 cm/4 in.

Head collar

A head harness comprising a nose-band, head-piece and throat lash, which is used for leading or tying up a pony.

Hock

The joint at the tarsus (ankle).

Jibbing

A refusal to go forwards.

Laminitis

A painful disease caused by the inflammation of tissues within the hoof. It can be recurrent.

Livery

Rent-paid accommodation, sometimes with daily care included.

Manger

A feed trough.

Near side

The pony's left side.

New Zealand rug

A tough waterproof rug for continuous use outdoors.

Numnah

A wool or cotton pad used under the saddle to relieve pressure and absorb sweat.

Off side

The pony's right side.

Palomino

A bright chestnut or gold body colour with a white mane and tail. In the USA, a recognized breed.

Pastern

The part of the foot between the fetlock and the hoof.

Piebald

Black and white patches on the coat.

Pommel

The raised front of a saddle.

Rig

A male with one undescended testicle.

Roan

A mixture of white and other coloured hairs evenly distributed over the body.

Roaring

A loud noise made by a galloping pony due to faults in the vocal chords.

Roller

A broad strap around the belly to keep a rug in position.

Sandcrack

A vertical split in the hoof wall.

Seedy toe

Bad smelling rot of the hoof wall.

Skewbald

Brown and white patches on the coat.

Snaffle

The commonest type of bit, usually with one ring on each side.

Snip

A small white mark on the nose.

Sock

White pastern and fetlock.

Sound

Healthy in all respects.

Speedy cut

A wound to one leg caused by contact with another when the pony is moving fast.

Stable rug

A rug used in the stable.

Stallion

An uncastrated male which is over three years of age.

Star

A white patch on the forehead.

Staring coat
A dull coat, often with the hairs standing up.
Strawberry
A pink-looking roan colour composed of a mix of chestnut and white hairs.
Surcingle
A strap going round the belly to fix a rug in place.
Tack
The equipment worn by a pony, including the saddle and bridle, etc.
Tendon
A gristly band of tissue that attaches a muscle to a bone.
Twitch
A stick with a loop of rope attached, which is used to twist a pony's upper lip and so compel it to stand still by inflicting pain. This should never be used.

Vice
A bad habit.
Wall eyed
Blue or blue and white eyes.
Warble
A fly that lays its eggs under a pony's skin. The grubs that hatch from the eggs produce lumps under the skin that eventually burst. This condition is less commonly seen, thank goodness, nowadays.
Weaving
A 'vice' in which a bored, stabled pony rocks its head and neck from side to side stereotypically.
Windgall
A puffy fluid-filled swelling above the fetlock which does not cause lameness.
Withers
The high point of the back, located at the base of the neck between the animal's shoulder blades.

USEFUL ADDRESSES

The British Horse Society
Stoneleigh Deer Park
Kenilworth
Warwickshire CV8 2XZ
Tel: 01926 707700
www.bhs.org.uk

British Horse Trials Association
(British Eventing)
NAC
Stoneleigh Park
Warwickshire CV8 2RN
Tel: 02476 698856
www.britisheventing.com

British Veterinary Association
7 Mansfield Street
London W1M 0AT
Tel: 0207 636 6541

Horses and Ponies Protection Association (HAPPA)
The Stables
Burnley Wharf
Manchester Road
Burnley
Lancashire BB11 1JZ
Tel: 01282 455992
www.happa.org.uk

The Pony Club of Great Britain
NAC
Stoneleigh Park
Kenilworth
Warwickshire CV8 2RW
Tel: 02476 698300

Riding for the Disabled Association
Lavinia Norfolk House
Avenue R
National Agricultural Centre
Stoneleigh Park
Warwickshire CV8 2LY
Tel: 02476 696510
www.riding-for-disabled.org.uk

Society of Master Saddlers UK Ltd
Kettles Farm
Mickfield
Stowmarket
Suffolk IP14 6BY
Tel: 01449 711642
www.mastersaddlers.co.uk

ACKNOWLEDGEMENTS

The publishers would like to thank the following people for their help in compiling this book:

Linzi Aiken BHSAI

Claire Baker BHSPI

Emma Bush

Claire Edwards

Melanie Hickey

Anita French of Culford Stables, Bury St Edmunds

Peter Hay of Bridlepath Saddlery, St John's Street, Bury St Edmunds, Suffolk IP33 1SN (Tel: 01284 754124)

INDEX

INDEX